Integration through Games and

to be returned on or before

Uwe Rheker

Integration through Games and Sports

Meyer & Meyer Sport

Original title:
Spiel und Sport für alle: Integrationssport für Familie, Verein und Freizeit
– Aachen: Meyer und Meyer Verlag, 1993
Translated by James Beachus

British Library Cataloguing in Publication Data
A catalogue record for this book is available from the British Library

Rheker, Uwe :
Integration through games and sports / Uwe Rheker. [Transl.: James Beachus].
– Oxford: Meyer & Meyer Sport (UK) Ltd., 2000
ISBN 1-84126-012-6

© 2000 by Meyer & Meyer Sport (UK) Ltd.
Oxford, Aachen, Olten (CH), Vienna, Québec, Lansing/Michigan, Adelaide, Auckland,
Johannesburg, Budapest
e-mail: verlag@meyer-meyer-sports.com
Translation: James Beachus
Cover Photo: Minkus Foto Design Agentur, Isernhagen
Cover design: Birgit Engelen, Stolberg
Cover and Type exposure: frw, Reiner Wahlen, Aachen
Editorial: Dr. Irmgard Jaeger, Aachen, John Coghlan
Typesetting: Times
Printed and bound in Germany
by Druckpunkt Offset GmbH, Bergheim
ISBN 1-84126-012-6

Index

Foreword

In recent years the need to be active in the sporting field has grown for those who have to live with a functional limitation as a result of a handicap, and this applies to children, youths and grown-ups alike. Organisations which have set themselves up to tackle this problem have contributed greatly towards the possibilities now offered to every disabled person, so that they have the freedom of choice to be able to be integrated into organised leisure sports. An example of this in Germany, the home country of the author, is seen in the numerous options offered by the Members Club of the Disabled Sport Union North Rhine Westphalia – a registered club (Mitgliedsvereine des Behinderten-Sportverbandes Nordrhein-Westfalen e.V. (BSNW)) working together with the German Disabled Sports Union (Deutscher Behinderten-Sportverband e.V. (DBS)).

As a principle, participation in group sport is based on the integration of a collection of like-minded persons – all interested in the same goal. Sporting activity remains the basic element of this integration.
It is exactly the family with disabled children that experiences isolation from society. Sport acts, in such a case, as a catalyst for the exchange of ideas between like-minded enthusiasts, be it playing together or simply experiencing things together. The opening is there not only for the disabled themselves, but also for each member of the family and family unit. The aim of group sports meets its target using the possibility of family sports activities.

The BSNW recognised early on that, following their experiences in sport for the disabled and sport for integrated groups, an extensive and complete understanding of sport in the first place was an absolute necessity, different from the traditional sport for the able bodied. It is a particular pleasure to see that these findings have now been described in full. This publication illustrates how sport can gain, if the experiences and possibilities from sport for the disabled are used.
    Furthermore the book makes a major contribution towards the idea of a natural and obvious co-operation between all people in society, and that exclusions – irrespective of their kind – are, at last, a thing of the past.

To quote from Uwe Rheker – "Everyone is valuable as a person just as he is, and not when and until he has reached some achievement in society". This thought, expressed by the author, underlines the ethical and moral basic principle on which this book is based.

BSNW will continue to encourage this development in future and, wherever it is necessary and possible, provide support. We hope that the suggestions and perspectives will be taken up by not only as many people as possible, but also by many clubs for the good of all people taking part in sport.

Duisburg February 1993   *Heinz Haep*
                        Behinderten-Sportverband Nordrhein-Westfalen e.V.

Foreword

The title of this book "Integration through Games and Sports" – dealing with the integration of sport for the family, club and leisure – already indicates what the prime aim of this publication is. The general actions of movement, games and sports activities by people with completely different abilities should be placed at the centre. There should be no exclusions according to performance, age, sex or handicap.

People with or without a disability, whether they be youths, grown-ups, girls, boys, men or women, foreigners or competitive sportsmen or simply leisure sports enthusiasts should all have the opportunity to experience what one can do together in games and sports. They will learn how to knock down barriers and prejudices, how to build up social contacts and how to get closer to ones fellow human beings.

This book is laid out to cover, above all, exercises for sport with disabled and able bodied people together and describes integrative "models", which have been proved in practice. In writing this book I am calling on more than ten years experience of integrated sport for the family, seven years experience in integrated wheelchair sports and approximately fifteen years experience in the faculty of 'movement, games and sports with disabled people' – a lot of which has been collected together from projects at the University and Polytechnic in Paderborn, Germany. The book aims to give a stimulus to all sorts of people engaged in sport, for heterogeneous groups and integrated sport, including that for the disabled. Where I have referred to activities in Paderborn and other German facilities, these serve to give examples of how these problems have been resolved there, and hopefully give tips for others throughout the world.

My thanks goes to all who have helped in the development of integrated sports and in the work involved in this book. Thanks first to my family, my wife Gisela and the children Rebekka Nan Hee, Tobias Ruben, Esther Swanni, Jonas Yong II and Rahel Terezinha. My thanks also goes to all those families who have stayed with us in our family sports group for ten years, and with who we have been able to have so much fun and joy together in sport and leisure activities.

Not least, I thank our students and scientific colleagues in the project 'movement, games and sports with disabled children and youths' at the University and Polytechnic in Paderborn – Achim Beule, Uli Purschke, Karl-Heinz Gottschalk and Hansi Dienst as well as all the team leaders and students who developed the ideas for games and introduced them. Thanks also goes to Maria Bock from our family sports group who has assembled the songs and rhymes in the English language for the games in this version of the book.

Paderborn February 1999   *Uwe Rheker*

Introduction

"Actions speak louder than words." (A. Lincoln, 1856)

This book is devoted to the integration of sport, that is to say joint sport between disabled and able bodied people. The main emphasis is laid on the description of the practice of integrated sport activities. Critical examination of this practice leads to a theory, which is constructively based on the various experiences gained during that practice. Integrated sport and the ensuing theory, by way of the various sports activities, have the aim together to change the attitude of disabled and able bodied people towards each other in a positive way. Not least of all the aim is to break down any social barrier towards disabled people.

A 'practice-oriented introduction to a varied pedagogical education for sport with the disabled and able bodied people' is given in **Chapter A**, and this follows on from a description of the social environment for disabled people, their families and their sport. Movement, games and sports give an opportunity for meeting up and provide the catalyst towards the integration of disabled people.

In the second part of this chapter, two different models for integrated sport are provided:

First of all "integration in family sport" is described. In Paderborn this is achieved by the integration of disabled people in local 'normal' sports clubs, with cross-pollination at all levels. Following on from this, the activity of the Paderborn 'Oak-Panther' children's wheelchair sports group is described. This sports club exists to further this activity in line with its charter.

Chapter B is devoted to the integration of sport in practice. First of all the various movements, games and sports activities are described. **Part 1** is devoted to sport for the whole family. Joint sport gives the opportunity for various different people of a heterogeneous group (people with or without a disability; children; youths; grown-ups; competitive sports enthusiasts and leisure sports enthusiasts ...) to grow together and develop into a group. In this way this chapter gives a stimulus for sport in such integrated sports groups as family sports groups, both with able bodied children, and family sports groups with disabled children and youths, leisure groups and so on and so forth.

Part 2 describes the different options for family sport, putting the individual at the centre, with all the varied interests and assumptions in the foreground. In this way, the heterogeneous target group is able to benefit and develop sport individually. In **part 3**, there is a description of sessions for integrated family sport, covering projects in which integrated sport is brought into a theme such as 'the circus' whereby all the activities concentrate on that theme. **Part 4** covers themes for activities outside the gymnasium – family leisure periods, swimming, hiking and fairs. Wheelchair sport is covered in **Part 5.**

Chapter C deals with the question of how to initiate, organise and finance integrated sports groups for disabled people.

Chapter D collects together all the games covered in the book and lists them in an index by category. This allows the reader to look up games according to the following criteria amongst others: location for the sport, form and organisation, aids and requisites for the games, activities, aims, experiences and criteria for suitability with wheelchairs. A separate game data bank has, in the meanwhile, been created, expanded on and improved. It contains more than 2,000 ideas for games that are divided according to over 40 different criteria and a plethora of various combinations which can be looked up. Individual games or data can be loaded, saved and printed out. For many of the games there is a multi-media version containing drawings, musical notes, music and videos.

A. THE THEORY OF INTEGRATION IN SPORT

I. The Social Environment for Disabled Persons, Their Families and Sport

1. Society

"Deeds are fruit and words are leaves." (Greek saying)

The Rights and Dignity of Man

Before we consider the question of integrated sport and its aims, we should first take a close look at our society in which disabled people and their children live. The examination does not intend to stereotype our society, but rather attempts to look at facets of society, as seen from the perspective of the disabled person.

We live in a society that affords all of its members the same basic rights. As expressed in the constitution – "The rights of man are inviolable"[1] – this forms a central basic principle. We live in a pluralistic society in which many different individuals are represented by their solidarity. Our society is therefore characterised as one in which all of its members act, or should act, in solidarity with each other.

Sharing in the Life of Society

Sharing in the life of society should be something open to all its members. It is quite unacceptable in the long run that a section of society (people in wheelchairs, cripples, parents with push-chairs and prams) are excluded by virtue of the way obstructions occur in the construction of public buildings such as town or council offices, post offices, in buses or on the railways. Society should not have to put up with such things.

In our society everyone should be able to develop into a responsible individual. This includes the opportunity to have the freedom of choice regarding school, training and education. In this respect many disabled children are not given full participation in society. They are often pushed off into special needs schools and kindergarten when many of them would be better placed in normal schools of their own choice. Unnecessary obstructions are placed in their path.

In Germany many of the Federal States have followed the example of rulings in Berlin. Disabled children and youths are able now to attend regular schools. For example, in the USA, where this is known as "mainstreaming", this provision goes without question (c.f. OPP 1993).

Since 1996, in North Rhine Westphalia, attendance at regular schools by disabled children has also been introduced. According to the laws for the advancement and further development of special needs requirements in schools "disabled children and youths can generally be accepted and taught in general schools" (KULTUSMINISTERIUM NRW 1995,1). Up until then they were only permitted to attend special needs schools.

Nevertheless with a plethora of obstacles and hurdles still to be overcome, it very often makes full participation in the life of society either very difficult, or even prevents this happening.

An Achievement-orientated Society

Our society centres itself around the 'achiever'. People who achieve, gain high recognition. Examples which show this are top sportsmen, top managers, successful businessmen etc.

This is why work and the workplace are graded highly in our society. The unemployed therefore feel themselves, justifiably, pushed aside. Just how disturbing the disabled feel about this aspect of a society of achievers is borne out in GUSTI STEINER's passage in his paper written in Berlin 1990 "The Disabled in Germany from 1945 to today". He illustrates their plight as follows: only when they are in a position to contribute something to society in their work will they have a chance to participate.

"Work, earn money –
these are the entrance tickets for participation in this society"
(STEINER 1990, 56).

He comes to this viewpoint, inter alia, by observing that the central theme of integration for disabled people is often being only in the workplace. Even in the Law of Rehabilitation in Germany integration speaks in the first instance about work and profession (See German Law of Rehabilitation Paragraph [1]).

This point is made even clearer in advice given to the Institute for Accident Insurance (Austria) regarding paraplegics:

"A paraplegic, who cannot be integrated into the workplace,
cannot be rehabilitated"
(STEINER 1990, 64).

It must be emphasised that this is not true. The value and dignity of the human being do not depend on his achievements!

> *"Everyone is valued as a person, just as he is,*
> *and not because of his achievements in society"*
> (RHEKER 1989a, 132).

The Term "Normal" in Society

In our society it was not only the "Hauptmann von Koepenick" that made the saying "clothes make the man" clear. Summing up people by their outward appearance allows us to come quickly to terms with each other, and it is quite understandable that we use this method first of all. It certainly has a role in our lives. Very often, however, we create a firm picture from these first external impressions, which is full of prejudices and does not do justice to the real person in front of us.

If we dress up in clothes that are not the 'in' attire, then we get noticed. In the same way all the other things about ourselves attract attention: the colour of the skin in coloured people, the non-European clothing worn by the Indians, Arabs and gypsies, people in wheelchairs, dwarfs and so on.

These things do not fit into the picture conjured up as 'norms' by society. They have been conceived for able bodied people – for 'normal' people. The disabled person therefore is mostly, and very often, overlooked and as a result lives in a world created by able bodied people, who have expectations of the particular roles to be played by everyone. Dependent on the degree of medical disability, many of the disabled are unable to fulfil these expectations in most of the areas of our society. The result is that even today, much that the able bodied take for granted, remains closed and unattainable for the disabled.

The departure from the 'norm'[2] – from normality – is often considered to be inferior. Able bodied members of society react with intolerance and disdain at "the diminished usefulness". The term "disabled" is therefore very often used to describe a condition and is placed in comparison to "normal". Disabled people are considered as "abnormal" and thus "are 'deviants'". In this a fictive majority depicts itself as a fictive "normality" (OFFERMANN 1986, 32).

The social definition of normality is mostly characterised by the average orientation regarding human behaviour and capabilities. A person is considered "normal" when they possess the average ability relative to the expectation of their role in society – they are able to fit into the existing system of norms and values. This viewpoint of normality lays the foundation for not being disabled, and from this the existence of the categorisation and stigmatisation[3] of the disabled. This form of attribution is not rare and is often therefore brought to the fore in order to demonstrate one's own qualities and capabilities in the background of a society that is based on principles of performance and competitive ability.

However, if one considers reality, one ascertains that hardly anyone fully comes up to the average norm. Differences are normal and occur often. Only a few people can match ideal norms of beauty, health and physical perfection, particularly those shown as normal in advertisements.

In spite of this people with visible physical abnormalities are effectively rejected and seen in a negative light (c.f. SEYWALD 1977, 35). This results in reactions ranging from offers of confused help to open discrimination. Disabled people present, to all extents and purposes, a threat to the system of norms, because they show up natural assumed values of health, beauty and performance as being false (c.f. SEYWALD 1977, 111). Therefore, at this juncture, it must be emphasised that the expression "normality" must be critically viewed as highly questionable. As a dynamic expression it should be considered in a changing light.

"It is normal to be different"

(von WEIZSÄCKER 1993).

It has been noticed that, in the last few years, initiatives in many walks of life have begun, which are committed to the needs of the disabled. All too often it simply has been a question of "doing something for someone". Most of these activities, however, are carried out often independent of the people they are meant for. The disabled person therefore does not have a chance to fully develop his ideas and interests because the activities are "steered by the helper". The aim of the responsible individual, as stated above, does not specifically come out on top. Preferable are activities that strive to create a partnership between the disabled and the able bodied.

It is often quite clear in the nomenclature, e.g., "sport with disabled children", that the disabled are equal partners. Unfortunately such integrated activities are mainly only "model attempts" (c.f. integration trials in schools in North Rhine Westphalia, Germany), which take place as "cases of authorised exceptions", or under particularly favourable conditions, or even under completely exceptional circumstances. The aim of these attempts at modelling is often to turn the co-ordination of disabled and able bodied persons into normality.

2.   Disablility

"Wrong words lead to war." (Chinese saying)

Do We Need the Term "Disabled"?

When one wants to describe joint co-operation between the disabled and able bodied taking part in sport and games, you have to carefully examine the term "Disability" or "disabled" and ask what it actually means and what the particular problems are that come from being disabled.

First of all I want to address the question whether it is necessary at all to define the term disabled. Do definitions of the description disability help, or do they perhaps even hinder in dealing with disabled people?

Many of the attempts to reach a definition are moulded by each different author's viewpoint, irrespective of whether they be on medical, sociological, educational or judicial grounds. When these definitions are seen in the context of the opposite to "norm", or as "not normal", they often cause the social exclusion of disabled people. Several descriptions are even discriminating: when terminology such as "lunacy" is still used as a medical definition one can certainly not describe this as being of any value.

A more accurate description of the individual types of disability, on the other hand, can be of value in assisting those able bodied persons in their dealings with the disabled by giving a relative orientation guide to the concrete disability.

As an example, a descriptive definition is necessary in the training of those dealing professionally (e.g., voluntary helpers, physiotherapists and sports supervisors) with the care of disabled people.

However, by categorising such people, this already leads to a particular pattern that tends to introduce prejudices from the very beginning.

Every disabled person, irrespective of the type of disability, is first and foremost an individual just like anyone else. The person is a special personality with varying and different characteristics which no other person possesses. Within the backdrop of the individual's point of view any attempt to provide a definition tends to be a limiting factor.

My experience, during the introduction of students to disabled sport for disabled children and youths, has shown that they (the students) often achieve more than their lecturers who have known the children and their disability problems for a long time. They deal with them without any prejudices even when they have no detailed information or specific knowledge of the disability possessed by their charges.

Terminology – up to now

The term "disability" has never been given a clear and generally accepted definition (c.f. SANDER 1990, 75). When one seeks a clear agreed description, one bumps repeatedly into different understandings and explanations.

According to RUNDE (c.f. RUNDE/HEINZE 1979, 9) there is no general and binding definition of the term "disability" that is free from question, aim or theoretical statement. He adds that there are varying and often conflicting sources for the assessment of a disability, and mentions for example medical diagnoses, personal opinion and wild estimates. On top of these are the defining levels of social-politics, sociology and education. RUNDE says that due to the variety of possible definitions used, disability is not a clearly definable phenomenon.

In getting to grips with the thematic let me attempt to give some definitions for the term "disability". From a judicial viewpoint disability is "not a temporary major impairment ..." (Bundessozialhilfegesetz (German Law for the Social Services) Article 124 Paragraph 4 – as in STORR 1985) defined as of a physical or mental nature ... "and independent from the cause ..."(Sozialgesetzbuch I, Article 10, in SGB 1989) results in a just claim for assistance.

In 1980, the World Health Organisation (WHO) undertook an attempt to reach an international and inter-disciplinary definition for the state of the disabled with the paper "International Classification of Impairments, Disabilities and Handicaps". In the paper a differentiation was drawn between: impairment as a loss or "anomaly concerning a psychological, physiological or anatomical structure or function ..." (Bundesminister für Arbeit und Sozialordnung (German Minister for Labour and Social Order) 1983, 4)), disability/loss of performance as "a (relevant to damage) limitation of an ability or the total inability to be able to carry out an action which is considered as normal for the human being ..." (Bundesminister für Arbeit und Sozialordnung (German Minister for Labour and Social Order 1983, 4), and disability as "... a disadvantage caused by damage or stemming from a reduced ability, which prevents certain people, either partially or totally, from carrying out a specific role which would be normal for that person after taking into consideration age, sex and social cultural factors" (SANDER 1990, 80).

THUST draws on the definition above and explains: "*A disability is a condition of irregularity lasting more than six months and which impairs or threatens to impair the afflicted person's integration in society as a result of a physical irregularity or a mental weakness or disturbance*" *(THUST 1980, 7).*

KLEE exercises harsh criticism on this and sees these "official" definitions as a discrimination against disabled people. A clear statement that the disabled person is not a human being like "you and me".

> *"Possessing an irregularity is not normal,*
> *does not conform and is simply abnormal"*
>
> (KLEE 1980, 11).

Moreover, THUST's definition speaks of an impairing disability in integrating with society. KLEE tries to correct this statement by writing:

> *"Of course the disabled want to be part of society, but they constantly bump up against*
> *the fact that society pushes them away, excludes them and isolates them"*
>
> (KLEE 1980, 11).

Because the term "disability" is quite variously portrayed in specialist literature, and because it is often couched in a berating and excluding manner, and is often prescriptive and describes the deviation from "normal", it is clear that there are only inadequate scientific attempts to find a definition for the disabled.

People with Disabilities

It is therefore more appropriate to express the term disability as 'that which proves to be realistically a hindrance'. SCHÖLER, in educational discussion on integration, makes the following suggestion: the term "disabled" should be replaced by the words "children and youths with hindrances", since, "the factor of the disability does not determine the whole personality, rather a disability is only one of many personality characteristics of a person" (SCHÖLER 1990, 84).

If we subscribe to this statement then we should exercise caution in our daily discriminative description of disabled, irrespective whether this occurs "only" as a rash oversight or through neglect.

When able bodied people are declared "healthy" in comparison to the disabled – often even spoken of by the disabled themselves – then there is a subconscious evaluation made which says that being disabled is a sickness; is the opposite to being healthy (KARL 1991, 35). disabled people can just as easily be "well" or "ill" as the able bodied.

Also the saying "chained to the wheelchair" is debasing and overdramatic for their occupants. Amongst the many people taking part in top sporting occasions in wheelchair basketball matches and on wheelchair marathons, I have never come across any of them who felt chained to their wheelchair. They can move themselves about in the wheelchair and can get practically anywhere when no obstacles are cropped up in their path.

There are people who are blonde, have a dark skin, wear spectacles or have some other disabilities that do not typecast the whole person, or cause that person to be, labelled by the disability. On the contrary these determine only a part of the personality. It is therefore preferable not to call a person disabled and thus stamp him as such. It is better to use the expression "disabled person" or "a person with this or that concrete individual disability".

The characteristic is not the disability. Rather more, the person is an individual, she is "Anna Bell" or he is "Jack Smith", who are coincidentally also disabled. The more we can recognise the person behind the disability and not the disability itself, the more we will be doing the disabled justice.

3.   Disabled Persons

"Auf Erden lebt kein Menschenkind, an dem man keinen Mangel find't"
(German saying).
("Upon this earth no child is perfect.")
"Variety is normal."

No One Is Perfect

"Since no one person is perfect, weakness and imperfection are characteristics of the human being"
(RHEKER 1989a, 132).

Everybody is constantly reminded of his limits and limitations in various areas:
• we age and do not live forever
• we tire,
• there are limits to our speed, our intellect, our body size, our strength ...
• with age our mobility lessens

From this point of view there are only gradual differences to disabled persons. In the case of a person in a wheelchair, for example, mobility is limited, or in the case of a mentally disabled person, the intellectual capability is not so good.

Disabled People Belong to a Humane Society

Disabled people belong to every "humane" society. In the same way that people whose possibilities are limited by age or illness still belong fully to society, disabled people belong also, irrespective of whether they were born disabled or became so through an accident or illness.

The more society does for the disabled, the more one sees also that disabled people belong to daily life. Anyone who has visited countries that are good examples of this (e.g., Sweden or the Netherlands) will have noticed this clearly.

By comparison, a Rumanian doctor told me once that in Rumania under Ceaucescu "there were no disabled people because they did not fit into the social system". One could not see any disabled people about. They were kept in homes, often in inhumane conditions.

The difficulty in obtaining any comparative material for the number of disabled persons in our society is well-known by those who have worked in this area before.

In Germany a start point is provided in the published data census of 1985 by the Sozialdata-Institut fuer Gesundheits- und Kommunikationsforschung (Social Data INSTITUTE FOR HEALTH AND COMMUNICATION RESEARCH). According to this the number of disabled persons in the FRG is estimated at an absolute figure of 7.8 million. This represents 13.54%. The SOZIALDATA INSTITUTE'S figures are considered in specialist literature as thoroughly reliable and realistic, not least of all because of a possible grey-area in the order of 25% (c.f. SCHUCHARDT 1987, 56 et seq., SPECK/MARTIN 1990, 33).

The figure of disabled persons, measured against the whole population, mean that every 10th citizen is a disabled person. This results in the fact that every citizen in our society has a disabled person in their immediate social environment.

However, this fact is often dismissed by many. Only when they are personally affected, or when they have broken down their prejudices concerning the disabled by virtue of becoming involved with someone they know, do they realise this factor.

There Is no Such Thing as the Disabled

Just as it was made clear in chapter 2, the disabled person is not defined by the disability as this is merely a part of his individual personality.

There is no such thing as *the* disabled, just as there is no such thing as *the* German, *the* Russian or *the* Black. One can and should always only speak of the disabled person who has this or the other disability; and of people who coincidentally possess the German or the Brazilian nationality or who have a dark skin colour.

There are many different disabilities which can manifest themselves in quite different ways. Thus amongst people, disabled by one of their senses, we have a range of impairments of vision and damaged vision through to blindness, and people with poor hearing to damaged hearing and deafness.

The term "physical disability" subsumes an abundance of various disabilities: amputation of parts of the leg (toes, foot, lower leg, upper leg, one leg or both legs); paraplegic (a whole host of variations); polio victims; spina bifida; limb deformations (dysmelia); arthritis, damage to the spinal cord; multiple sclerosis; cerebral palsy with various different degrees of spastic paralysis; athetosis and ataxia, etc.

In a similar way terms to do with mental ability fall into different categories concerning mentally disabled persons. On top of this come the various terms for the educationally disabled. The mentally disturbed form a further large group which has to be viewed differently. A very non-uniform picture with many very individual differences is formed in describing people with more than one disability e.g., a blind and mentally disabled child.

Sitting on the periphery of disabled conditions are the chronic sick and people with organic illnesses such as cardiovascular disorders, diabetes, asthma, rheumatism etc.

Thus there are several reasons why the term "the disabled" should not be used:
- There are many very varied types of disability.
- For every type of disability there are different expressions for categories or degrees of the disability, which are often not at all comparable with each other (c.f. degree of disability in competitive sports).
- The use of such terms often implies some form of stereotyping – "stamping" , or a "sorting" into different pigeonholes, and this can encourage exclusion and isolation of disabled people rather than the opposite.
- The weightiest reason for avoiding such a categorisation, however, lies in consideration of the personality of the disabled person. The actual disability or affliction is merely one part of the personality. It should not completely colour the image of the whole of the personality.

Disabled People in Society

In our society, which has been described and characterised earlier as being as an 'achievement-orientated society', the possibility for the disabled person to be able to operate and to develop and realise himself as an individual is extremely limited. This ranges from spatial barriers, moves on to cover unsuitable workplaces afforded to the disabled, and ends up with the isolation of extreme and multiple disabled from society.

Thus most of the disabled people cannot reach a top post in a profession or in society. An exception here of course is SCHÄUBLE, previously the CDU-party-whip when they were in power. He reached his position in party politics before he was injured by an assassination attempt which left him disabled.

In top positions in politics, professional careers and in the management of leisure activities (e.g., unions, clubs and so on) disabled people are not well-represented apart from a few exceptions. Their concerns have to be represented by specially appointed persons, so that their interests do not suffer. This is why there are such appointments to cover the disabled issues in government, universities and industry, etc.

Similarly disabled people are more often excluded rather than integrated in educational or leisure activities. They are incarcerated into kindergarten and schools for children with special needs or workshops for the disabled. There are also special homes, asylums or hostels and sports clubs for the disabled. Thanks to all the criticism, however, it must be said that these special facilities have emphasised (in the case of special needs schools) the basic principle that these people are capable of learning, and this has now been brought out into the open.

The prejudices and barriers, in relation to the disabled, can only be broken down by affording the possibility offered by joint activity such as seen in integrated kindergarten, schools and leisure activity clubs.

The integration of the disabled into our society can only be improved by ensuring the existence of more possibilities for interactivity between the disabled and the able bodied.

4.   Able Bodied Persons

"There are short and long fingers – one cannot stretch them all to be the same length."
(Vietnamese saying)

Participation in Daily Life in Society

Unlike the disabled, the able bodied are able to participate fully in society. They are able to have a free choice of kindergarten, school and profession. They are able to pursue almost all their own interests and their liking and preferences in sport and leisure, etc. They are not placed in homes or workshops. On the contrary they can seek out their own residence and workplace by themselves. In society the way is open for them to be able to take on various functions and thereby advance both professionally and socially.

They rarely take the opportunity to have contact with disabled people. We have to really go into basics in order to come up with an answer to the question of why we must particularly consider the attitude of society towards the disabled.

The Attitude towards Disabled People

Because of the protective blanket thrown around us, even from kindergarten age, and despite experience of living shoulder to shoulder, able bodied people know far too little – sometimes even nothing – about the characteristics, problems and daily life of their disabled fellow human beings. This lack of knowledge leads to the rejection of the disabled and they are perceived as different and strange in the negative sense. Most able bodied people do not know how to react when confronted by a disabled person and therefore react with fear and insecurity (c.f. CLOERKES 1979, 440 et seq.).

Alongside the ignorance about the disabled there is unfortunately an influence still prevalent today that has its historical roots in a hostile behavioural pattern[4]. Even today disability is often considered as a punishment for a sin or the breaking of a taboo. Several empirical studies into people's understanding of the term "disability" confirm the prejudices covered above.

The social conditions for disabled people in Germany are still characterised by rejection, exclusion and social distancing (c.f. BECKER 1988, VON BRACKEN 1976, CLOERKES 1985, JANSEN 1981, SPECK 1988). "Just as before one can reckon to be confronted with a clearly negative attitude. Social integration would find real limitations as a result"(SPECK 1988, 303).

From the studies, however, the following must be noted:
> "According to the type of disability, considerably different attitudes to the disabled exist. Able bodied react more favourably to disabled people who are physically disabled or who have an impaired sense. People who have a very pronounced visible disability [....] are just as correspondingly severely rejected as the mentally disabled" (CLOERKES 1979, 180).

Scientific statistics show that the extent of peoples' knowledge is very thin.

VON BRACKEN (1976) came to the conclusion, as a result of a survey, that there was a considerable lack of knowledge in people's minds concerning mentally disabled children. He also established that, in some cases superstitious attitudes towards the origin and causes of the disability were rife. Most of those asked believed that alcoholism, inbreeding and hereditary were the most common causes, and that mental disability was the worst disability one could meet. Disabled children were seen as weird and were met with horror, fear and disgust. Social distancing was clear in such cases where people would not let their children play with a mentally disabled child. Two thirds of the people questioned expressed the opinion that it would be better if disabled children were kept in a home. Also 43.5% suggested that all mentally disabled children should be kept in homes. The most shocking conclusion to the questionnaire was an overriding opinion that it would be better if mentally disabled children were to die early. The study showed, moreover, that among those asked, who personally knew a mentally disabled child, the social distance was less and their emotional attitude was more positive (c.f. VON BRACKEN 1976, 278).

In a questionnaire about physical disabilities, conducted by JANSEN in 1981, he established that able bodied people were poorly informed about their disabled colleagues. For example the majority of those asked did not know at all what constituted a disability, and many were not able to differentiate between a disability and sickness. The ability of a physically disabled person was generally estimated as being poor.

Answers to questions regarding the most common cause of a disability often, to a certain degree, blamed the parents for reasons such as misuse of alcohol, smoking or attempts at abortion amongst others (c.f. JANSEN 1981, THIMM 1977).

CLOERKES (c.f. 1979, 315) is particularly critical of this last conclusion from the questionnaire. He sees that ".... the commonest assumption of the causes notably centres on 'discrimination'. There is almost a concerted attempt to stigmatise parents of disabled children".

Even if the study material, being somewhat old, has to be treated with certain circumspection, more recently conducted statistics by other scientists do not show any appreciable differences of opinion on the subject.

SEIFERT (1984) concluded in his research, concerning the attitude to disabled people, that "contact with the mentally disabled was the category which was most rejected" (MAIKOWSKI/PODLESCH 1990, 261). In one of his questionnaires more than half agreed with the point that the physically disabled "were to be seen as lacking in ability (weak, sick, tired) and in need of help, as well as sensitive, distrustful, irritable – aggressive and timid – insecure human beings" (SEIFERT/STANGL 1981, 79). SEIFERT, like VON BRACKEN, unfortunately had to come to the conclusion that the majority of people questioned were in agreement that physically disabled people should be in homes (SEIFERT/STANGL 1981, 101). BAECHTHOLD (1984, 7), in his research, is able to confirm the statement, with a statistic of almost 90% agreeing, that many people feel unsure of themselves (SEIFERT/STANGL 1981, 94), and makes the remark:

"Feelings of repulsion are present in almost a fifth of the population. The main problem with the distancing of people's emotions lies in the insecurity felt by them, and was listed as such by approximately 70%."

Attitudes and reactions like these above stand in the way of a partnership and co-existence between the disabled and the able bodied. So that I do not appear to be biased, at this juncture I wish to emphasise that there are many people in our society who actually do have a partnership relation with the disabled. However, negative attitudes still prevail and are just asking for modification.

Possibilities for Contact with Disabled People

When we go over the results of research into the attitude of society to disabled colleagues and think of how we can break down the prejudices and social distancing of disabled people, we can only come to the conclusion and opinion that the "non-integration" of disabled people must be changed as quickly as possible.

Regarding the question of how, there is an answer in two parts that helps towards making an unprejudiced solution. On the one hand, the vague terminology used in connection with the disabled must be replaced by positive information. On the other hand we must strive to increase the contact between able bodied and disabled people.

It is quite obvious that contact should begin at as early an age as possible – as early as pre-school when no prejudices have yet been established. These facts call for kindergarten without segregation; for integrated kindergarten and for the integration of as many disabled children into the so-called "normal kindergarten". In addition to the necessary special needs schools open to choice, in respect of other schools one should take steps to allow disabled children to attend normal classes. The few "integrated model classes" are, in part, only an alibi and contain far too few children – many more would wish to study in integrated classes.

A further area where much more integration could be realised is in the training period following on from school age and in professional training.

An important area in life, where social integration could be realised, is where one lives. If less disabled people living in large homes, mostly situated far from the residential areas of the "normal" citizens, were allowed to live in small groups amongst the normal residential districts, there would be a better chance for them to be integrated into daily social life.

Leisure activities also offer a number of possibilities for joint co-operation between disabled and able bodied people. Sport provides a possibility that will figure strongly in the passages that follow. Further possibilities also spring to mind such as the area of culture, hobbies, evening classes, dancing, festivals and fairs etc.

5.   Family

"To be related to one another is not enough; one must also wine and dine together."
(Zimbabwean saying)

What Is a Family?
Before we get down to cover sport in the family in chapter II, we must first of all have a look at the term 'family' and what it really means. This does not mean we have to examine the subject from a scientific or all-embracing point of view – more on a descriptive phenomenological level.

Well then – what is a family?

The family is the smallest social community in our society. It is the unit in which our first social experiences are made. A fundamental characteristic of the family is the parents-child relationship. It is as a small child, a baby, totally helpless in the loving acceptance of the parents, that we experience the first future social affinities. The family is, therefore, as in the words of sociologists, the 'primary factor of socialisation'.

Education
In order that a child can develop into a responsible mature individual it is dependent on education. Through education the child is changed from an irresponsible helpless being into someone totally responsible for his or her actions. This subjective aim in education is also called emancipation. As a basis, it is supported by the right of the individual to be able to develop his personality. The right of the development of the individual belongs to the child, and just as much, to the parents.

Furthermore, a family is characterised by the factor of social co-existence, which primarily means the co-existence of different generations (parents-child and sometimes grandparents) and sexes (man/woman and boy/girl). Social relationships on the same level of a generation (brothers and sisters) also play an important role in the social form of the family.

The Function of the Family in Society
In answer to the question of the function of the family in our society, there are of course, dependent on scientific approach or philosophy, a number of quite different opinions.

The following basic statements can be made as a generalisation of the differing approaches:

- The family is the foundation for the preservation of the population and society.
- For the children – the up-and-coming generation – the family is the breadwinner, the clothier, the setter of standards ...
- The children are a guarantee for old-age care and support for the parent's generation.
- The family functions as a provider for all those things which are not provided by social authorities, or those things they do not need to provide such as kindergarten, schools, churches etc.

Indeed, the achievements of the family for the next generation are generally very poorly recognised by society, and this area is very underdeveloped. Similarly the family's participation in society is limited and also borders on financial dependency, especially for those with several children or little ones. Regarding cultural or social events like the theatre, concerts, carnivals etc., the financial burdens are such that they have to forego them. The same applies to journeys by air, skiing holidays, club subscriptions, commercial offers such as fitness studios, and so on.

When the children are young, and during their illnesses, the parent's leisure activities are greatly reduced. Families with disabled children experience these limitations more intensively than parents of able bodied children.

6.   The Family with Disabled Children

"Because God could not be everywhere, he created mothers."

(Arabian saying)

The Burden of the Family with Disabled Children

Families with disabled children bear a considerably higher burden than families with able bodied children. Similarly the care and nursing of disabled children is extremely time-consuming. Incentive measures and attending therapy exercises come on top of all the other things. Concerning care and nursing, families with severely disabled children find themselves particularly tied to this all their lives.

As a result families with disabled children are more heavily stretched as the primary factor of socialisation than families with able bodied children.

Besides the school exercises, very often attendance at different sorts of therapy has to be kept up: physiotherapy, riding as a therapy, game therapy, music therapy, swimming, psychomotor treatment, and so on.

Because many disabled children are often not independent enough to attend the therapy treatment classes on their own, one of the parents has to bring, accompany and fetch the child to and from these events. The mother is mainly hit by this requirement, as shown in the following survey carried out by the Paderborn Group[5].

Table No. 1

Question No 24: The following people accompany me to the sports classes.

– Mother	98 N	30.63%
– I go on my own	53 N	16.56%
– Father	39 N	12.19%
– Brother or sister	35 N	10.94%
– Friends	27 N	8.44%
– Social worker/volunteer	25 N	7.81%
– School friend	23 N	7.18%
– Others	20 N	6.25%

(N = 320 people asked in survey – multiple answers were possible)/ As at 12/91.

This leaves very little time for the parents of a disabled child to follow their own leisure activities.

The Function of the Family with Disabled Children in Society

The development of the disabled child's personality occurs primarily within the family circle. Besides taking care of the welfare and nursing of a disabled child, for the most part, the family also has to take care of the child's stimulation and therapy requirements.

The social co-existence of disabled and able bodied children in a family can serve as a 'living model', exemplifying social co-habitation of differing social groups in society in general.

In a humane society responsibility and solidarity are important elements of the attitude and behavioural pattern towards those not so well-blessed in their capability. In this way the family with a disabled child is a living example of the way to go about this. The 'weak' and the 'lame' both belong in our human lives. Therefore disabled people belong to a humane society.

Participation in Social Life

In the passage describing the burdens which beset a family with disabled children, it was made clear that the challenges and time factor faced by parents allowed them very little time and space for themselves to be able to take part in society. On the one hand this is valid for parents, but on the other hand it also affects the whole family.

Very often able bodied brothers and sisters are most particularly affected by these limitations. The necessary parental time for them, which they should be afforded, is simply not available. There is also less time for joint activities by the whole family.

If families come across rejection or some other negative experience when they are participating with their disabled children in the few joint activities that are available open to the public, then they often withdraw further into themselves. Thus the social isolation increases, not only for disabled children, but also for families with disabled children.

7. Children and Youths

> *"Little streams all eventually flow together to make the big rivers."*
>
> *(French saying)*

Children as Independent Personalities

If you could follow the development of a child from birth, you would agree with me that children are individual personalities "right from the beginning". In 1991, the Berlin professor of educational science, HANS-LUDWIG FRESSE described children as "little philosophers" at the Congress of the German Paediatrics Society.

> *"Already at an age of about five years children begin to ask abstract questions about time. Their search for understanding is accompanied by a feeling of astonishment and wonderment over the puzzle and mystery – something that Aristotle would have called the beginning of philosophy."*
>
> (DPA report 1991)

From my experiences with my own children I know that children always continually want to get down to basics and pose the question "Why?". If one gets involved in answering one comes into astonishingly deep discussions even with pre-school or primary school aged children. My son Jonas, aged 5, discusses with me all sorts of imaginable things, even the "meaning of life", for hours on end, and quite deeply too.

In the first few days following birth, brothers and sisters show differences in the way that they make contact with their environment, how they show their feelings, their needs (hunger) and their reactions to love and affection. Later on children develop quite different personal characteristics and interests; each child develops into an individual personality. To the same degree this applies to able bodied as well as disabled children. The following axiom is therefore surely true:

> *"Everyone has the right to develop his or her own individual capability. Development of the personality and its stimulation does not depend on the variety of 'appearance' of the person. Logically LÖWISCH [6] sees it as "massively inhuman" e.g., to deprive a mentally disabled person on account of his appearance"*
>
> (RHEKER 1989a, 132).

The demand made in chapter 1 that everyone in our society, whether disabled or not, should have the chance to develop to be a responsible individual, matches the basic right of being able to develop one's capability individually. Only then can he develop and gain the ability to act in all areas of life, and thus be independent, and later be able to construct his own life.

Bringing up the disabled child to be independent becomes a very important aim. Very often it is necessary to take this in small steps and continually give encouragement so that the individual personality of the child is strengthened to the point where it has the confidence to do what it really can. Very often the development of independence is hindered by overprotection or even, on the other hand, overstretch. The whole subject of 'movement, games and sports', and in particular swimming, is an ideal area for the furtherance of independence.

Everyone in our society has a right to an upbringing. This is my demand, as I state in the fourth principle of my dialectical approach to the educational theory of sport for the disabled, as follows:

> *"Every person has the right to live and be happy in the community. This means also that no one should be ostracised from society, or simply be forced to assimilate social graces for the sake of conforming. Everyone must be afforded the opportunity – by colleagues and by society itself – to be able to partake fully in social life"*
>
> (RHEKER 1989a, 132).

Only in this way can solidarity with the weaker ones, and consideration for those not so capable etc., be exercised. The attainment of these social aims in the education of disabled and able bodied children and youths (as well as grown-ups of course) is equally important and significant.

Limited Participation in Social Life

The dependence of children and youths, both socially and financially, on their parents and grown-ups makes it obvious that they have only a limited participation in social life until they come of age. Children are kept to fixed times to be home (in the evening), so they do not have the opportunity to undertake all leisure activities as freely as grown-ups do.

Children and youths show an increase in becoming 'student workers', jobbing even during school time in order to gain financial independence. This shows their desire for an even greater degree of financial independence. For some youths there is very little time, besides school and a job, to follow their interests and talents.

8.   Leisure

"If one has a hobby this enhances the value of life" (Saying)

What Is Leisure?

We live in a society in which leisure takes on an ever increasing and important role. One can even speak of an increasingly 'leisure-oriented society'.

Society sees leisure as part of the schedule with work (obligation and time spent taking orders) and leisure time (time for self-determination and freedom). Relatively, as work hours became less, the desire for a counter-balance – relaxation – grew. Today leisure is not seen as the opposite to work. On the contrary it is considered a separate part of life. It means time which is free of compulsion and dependence, and which can be used for one's individual and social wishes.

OPASCHOWSKI interprets leisure with its full meaning as "free time, ... which is characterised by that time which is free from commitments and duties" and which allows "freedom of choice, conscious decisions for oneself and permits socialising" (c.f. OPASCHOWSKI, 1982, 2).

The Meaning of Leisure

According to the definitions given above, leisure means one has time available for self-development; one has the freedom of choice over a variety of activities and thus is able to take one's own decisions regarding interests, desires, wishes and abilities.

Thus leisure is an ideal arena for activity and training on the path of the 'immature child' to the 'responsible individual'. Leisure offers many possibilities to practice socialising. Leisure can be carried out within the family circle, with friends, in various groups or in a club, or it can be carried out on one's own.

The study by BRETTSCHNEIDER/BRÄUTIGAM in 1990, "Sport in der Alltagswelt von Jugendlichen" ("Sport in Everyday Life of Youths"), makes the point that the overriding characteristic in today's youth leisure scene is the socialising aspect. Considering what one can do in leisure activities, there are two forms – active and passive. The latter category includes so-called 'market force' activities such as listening to music, television, radio, watching theatre and spectating at cultural or sporting events.

Active leisure activities cover rather more creative or productive actions such as reading, playing a musical instrument, acting, painting, making a film, sport, sauna, fitness studio training, visiting a solarium, hiking, going for a swim, attending the youth group, working for a political party, church activities, working for the 'Third World' etc. In all of these one's own activity and participation is the uppermost consideration in the leisure activity.

The importance of leisure manifests itself not only by an increase in the variety of possibilities, but also by a quantitative increase in 'free time' available for it. Shorter working hours, the influence of different forces such as industry, economical restructuring, tourism and the mass media, as well as scientific advances have led to this enormous increase in importance of leisure, not only for the individual but for society as a whole. In 1900 the working week was 61.5 hours. From 1955, when the working week was 48.8 hours, it reduced to 38.9 hours by 1989 (c.f. HOF 1989, 172, INSTITUT DER DEUTSCHEN WIRTSCHAFT KÖLN 1990, 15 (Institute for German Economy)). A working week of 35 hours is being aimed at in the future.

Increased free time has demonstrably led to an equitable increase in supply and demand in the leisure sphere. Complete leisure industries have developed and this has led to new careers such as leisure sports teachers, entertainment hosts, fitness studio managers, health advisers, club managers and coaches etc.

Leisure and Sport

The possibilities of taking part in a sporting leisure activity have become more varied and have continually increased. You can see this development in what is offered by sports clubs. For a long time now the tendency towards 'mono sport' (e.g., only soccer) has been disappearing to be replaced by clubs offering a variety of sporting leisure activities. Besides traditional sports such as gymnastics, swimming, soccer, handball, volleyball, basketball and table tennis amongst others. Fitness training, ski gymnastics, relaxation training, spinal cord exercises and similar are being increasingly offered.

Some sports clubs are branching out into new areas and turn not only to their members but offer beyond these a system of courses for non-members. Examples are water gymnastics, recreational sport, parents-child groups, spinal cord exercises, yoga and other relaxation technique exercises. This can also be seen in the curriculum of evening classes where there is a tendency to offer a larger degree of leisure and health sports subjects.

Leisure and the Family

Increased free time does not at the same time mean that families with children have more time for joint ventures. Quite the opposite happens and there is more of a drift away from each other as each member of the family strives to develop and realise his or her own interests. Because there is little opportunity in school or in one's profession to develop personal interests because of the set work and duties, leisure time is used for self-realisation.

This means that in families with children, one goes off to play tennis while the other goes to music school, or one meets with friends to play computer games and the other prefers to go on a bike ride. Watching television, going to the theatre, swimming, disco, club sport, coffee parties, shopping and leisure sport are a few of the divergent free time activity alternatives.

When each member wants to pursue his interests on his own, and simply develops his own personal capabilities, there is often never much time left for joint activities in the family circle. Therefore families, especially with several children, should attempt to set joint targets for their leisure time e.g., as is possible in family sport.

Using my own family as an example, let me show you how one can still realise individual personality and capability in coming together for different leisure time activities. Here are the children with their differing interests.
- Rahel (six years old): ballet and kindergarten
- Jonas (eleven years old): Tae Kwon Do; table tennis; communion classes; primary school
- Esther (fourteen years old): piano; youth group; Rudolf Steiner school with additional activities like theatre; choir etc.
- Tobias (fifteen years old): cathedral choir; basketball; Rudolf Steiner school with additional activities like theatre; choir etc.
- Rebekka (seventeen years old): basketball; school choir; baby-sitting; high school

On top of these, there are the different activities for myself and my wife in the "Third World Workshop", advisory work in the Terre des Hommes group, leader of various disabled persons swimming sports groups, engagement in integrated wheelchair and family sports, and amongst many other activities, such as the parish family group, jogging, learning Portuguese, committee work with the "Sao Paulo Aids Help Organisation".

The mutual connection is the activity which the whole family can participate in such as family sport, swimming, leisure time activities with the various disabled peoples sports groups, the "Third World Work" and music.

Picture 1: The children in an "integrated" family with their individual sporting leisure time activities (together for family sport)

9.   Leisure and the Family with Disabled Persons

"If at first you do not succeed, try, try, try again." (old saying)

The Disadvantages of the Disabled in Their Leisure Time

"The social integration of the disabled takes place to a large extent during leisure time activities."
(Deutscher Bildungsrat (German Department of Education) 1973)

Although, generally, there is an abundance and variety of leisure activities on offer, there is very little opportunity for the disabled, or families with disabled children and youths, to avail themselves of them adequately.

OPASCHOWSKI (1976, 130) and KERKHOFF (1982, 6 et seq.) have both stated that there is a disadvantage to disabled groups in their leisure activities. Many existing "leisure activities on offer for the disabled are either very limited in their suitability or simply rarely accessible" (ZIELNOK/SCHMIDT-THIMME 1979, 25). Often qualified personnel and assistant care personnel are not there, as well as suitable premises and transport.

The key factor in the exclusion of disabled people from normal leisure activities is often the social distancing of the able bodied from the disabled. Many able bodied people are unsure of themselves in the company of the disabled and tend as a result to shut them out (see the results of the survey by JANSEN 1974 and VON BRACKEN 1976). In the company of the disabled, the able bodied are more likely to feel as if they are the 'disabled'!

If we want to change this situation, dismantle the prejudices and close the social gap, then, besides ensuring a flow of positive information about the disabled, we must make sure that there are possibilities for the disabled and able bodied to meet, so that they can undertake something together. In this way fears and prejudices can be overcome and new understanding and experience gained which permit unbiased co-operation.

Leisure Activities for Disabled People

Leisure activities for disabled people have a twofold shortfall:
- Compared with able bodied people there are fewer leisure activities on offer. There are fewer possibilities for disabled people to organise actively their leisure time themselves. There are only the offerings of responsible bodies such as schools, homes or workshops for disabled people. Evening classes only offer occasional courses for disabled people such as "reading, writing and arithmetic" or special dancing classes for the disabled. As a result a large part of the participation in leisure activity is rather more of a passive nature, such as watching television or listening to music etc.

- There are hardly any offers of "integration" that further the cause of the disabled meeting the able bodied. The majority of "leisure activities" are specifically only for the disabled. The disabled do not get to meet the able bodied. This is borne out by the results of a "survey by a project group with mentally disabled people in Paderborn (Germany) concerning leisure and work for the disabled." One of the aims of most of the things on offer was "integration"

"Nevertheless, in practically all things on offer, one did not come across a able bodied person, apart from the voluntary or occasional worker. The majority of offers took place in the margins, away from the central business"

(MICHELS 1988, 20).

How leisure activities can contribute excellently towards the social integration of disabled people, however, is shown in the next passage.

Leisure as a Sphere for Social Integration

The significance of leisure in the social integration of disabled people is undisputed in specialised literature (see Deutscher Bildungsrat (German Department of Education) 1973, 106; ZIELNIOK/SCHMIDT-THIMME 1979, 89). It has been successfully proved, time and time again, by the presence of many practical activities such as holiday leisure activities and sports events.

The following table shows the results of a survey by KERKHOFF in 1980, and confirms the opinion of the experts that the opportunities for integration in the leisure sphere are rated as high:

Table No. 2 (c.f. KERKHOFF 1982, 23)

The chance of integration in the following fields:		
	– in the workplace	13.3%
	– in politics	3.1%
	– in primary or secondary school	12.6%
INTEGRATION	**– in leisure time**	**47.6%**
	– in none of the above	2.9%
	– undecided	19.3%
	– other answers	1.2%
(N = 420 people asked in survey)		100.0%

Despite the high rating given to the significance of leisure time for the social integration of disabled people, in reality the number of measures to achieve integration is up until now still very low. Even though the number of activities encompassing integration has increased lately, the real demand for jointly organised leisure activities is in no way covered enough.

Similar results came from a survey of experts by ZIELNIOK/KLOECKNER "Expertenbefragung zur Freizeitförderung im Bereich der Rehabilitation Behinderter" ("Development of Leisure Activities in the Area of Rehabilitation of the Disabled") (ZIELNIOK/SCHMIDT-THIMME 1979, 88 et seq.).

Nevertheless, the majority of those asked saw that "there was preferential treatment given to the disabled in leisure activities with regard to integration, communication and social experience. Activities in leisure time should bring the disabled out of their isolation and make meetings with others, disabled and able bodied, possible."

The urge for social contact during their leisure time is firmly placed in the foreground by the majority of disabled as well as able bodied people. In order to give this thesis its correct credence, new studies concerning the construction of leisure time for the disabled must be put in place.

A survey is underway at the University and Polytechnic of Paderborn in Germany covering the conduct of sport for disabled children and youths, led by Professor Wolf-Dietrich BRETTSCHNEIDER and Sports Teacher Uwe RHEKER. The following two tables show the interim results of questions to disabled children and youths regarding especially the subject of "motivation".

Table No. 3

This shows the "Top Ten" regarding the driving force behind sport for disabled children and youths[7]. "In sports I want to:"	
– have fun	4.65
– do something together with others	4.33
– do something for my health	4.13
– increase my performance	3.95
– do something different	3.91
– make friends	3.89
– consciously do something for my fitness	3.75
– belong to a group of friends	3.73
– have a 'fling'	3.65
– relax	3.17
(N = 239 people asked in survey)	As at 12/91

Table No. 4

This table illustrates the 'importance of sport' for disabled children and youths. "importance":		
- something very important which I do not want to forego under any circumstances	65 N	27.20%
- something important but I can keep it down to limits	71 N	27.71%
- various interests which are just as important as sport for me	49 N	20.50%
- sport plays no role in my life	4 N	1.67%
- no details	50 N	20.92%
(N = 239 people asked in survey)	As at 12/91	

These tables, with 54.9% (136 votes), show clearly that movement, games and sports play a role ranging from "important" to "very important" as a leisure pastime for disabled children and youths. Against the backdrop of these figures, the subject of "movement, games and sports" can be seen as considerably fitting in providing the catalyst for disabled children and youths to meet.

Sport as a Leisure Activity for the Disabled

ZIELNIOK/KLOECKNER's survey also shows that "movement, games and sports" is one of the most important leisure activities for disabled people.

> *"The area of 'sport and games' is, by far, at the top of those named in the facilities offering existing leisure activities"*
> (ZIELNIOK/SCHMIDT-THIMME 1979, 89).

Despite this fact the number of disabled people participating in sport in their leisure time is extremely low.

According to statistics from the DSB (German Sports Union) 34.5% of able bodied people are organised into a sports club. The figure for children and youths lies at a much higher percentage. In NRW, according to inquiries made by BRETTSCHNEIDER/ BRÄUTIGAM (1990, 171), approximately 54% of male and about 38% of female youths were in sports clubs (an average across the sexes of 46%).

If we look at the figures of disabled people taking part in sport, it is clear in the first instance that there is a glaring requirement for improvement as well as the fact that the motto of the DSB – "sport for all" – is in no way yet realised.

Of the 7.8 million disabled people (in Germany) only 197,000 are registered as members with the DBS (German Disabled Sports Union)– which is just short of 3%. In NRW the figure is as low as 2.8% – that means 65,000 disabled people.

Even if these figures are not quite reliable, they still show the large improvement necessary in the possibilities for movement, games and sports for disabled people in particular, especially for children and youths. It is exactly this group, as opposed to able bodied adolescents, who only have limited opportunities to participate in movement and sports activities in a non-organised form. Most disabled children and youths do not manage to fit into "normal" sports groups, even when they are not primarily performance-oriented.

The lack of possibilities in the area of "integrated sports" is assessed as being considerably larger. There are so-called "models" that promote in particular the joint participation of disabled and able bodied in movement, games and sport. There is, however, a long way to go to the integration of sport as "normal sports activity between disabled and able bodied people".

Similarly disabled people are seldom included in non-sporting leisure activities. There are very few youth groups, such as the Scouts for example, that attempt to integrate disabled children and youths into their organisations. However it is generally left to individual efforts. The integration of the disabled in "normal leisure activity" being one exception.

Family sport with disabled children is a good opportunity for disabled people to mix in the activities of the able bodied or vice versa. Integrated sport with the disabled, even if planned as a model, can and should be something normal. It should lead to the natural co-operation between disabled and able bodied (c.f. RHEKER 1991c, 79 et seq.). This will be illustrated by examples to do with family sport and integrated wheelchair sport covered in the second part of this chapter.

10. Sport

"Fear not to go forward slowly, but fear should you stand still."
(Taiwanese saying)

In the following passages about the phenomenon of sport there is an emphasis placed on those aspects that are particularly relevant to integrated sport.

Importance of Sport in Society

Sport in our society has become a phenomenon that is continually gaining in importance. Seen as something of a "minor consideration" it has long become something of a "major consideration" for many. This is seen not only in professional sport where already horrendous sums are paid out in prizes, but also in the hugh increase in the leisure and sports industry with commercial fitness studios and similar things appearing.

The development of this in sport increases, and efforts are often sponsored by many scientific research organisations. As a result top sportsmen and women are being advised and sponsored by sports doctors, specialists in biomechanics, training specialists and sometimes also by psychologists. On top of this there is also the scientific optimisation of sports equipment by competent scientific institutes. World championships, the olympic games, national championships, soccer league games all fascinate the masses and week by week these have turned into mass media events. Also, in everyday life there is an increase in the importance of movement, games and sport. The role of sport in our generally passive world grows in its importance. Sport achieves the balance between a lack of movement and activity in the workplace and an excess of too many passive leisure interests. Sport has become a significant factor in the world of leisure.

On the one hand, sport mirrors society's 'norms' of achievement, while on the other it creates a balance to the normal everyday things and the narrowing world of work by opening up new avenues of other types of sport such as mountain climbing, diving, surfing etc.

Sporting Values

Sport offers itself to the transmission of values to the individual and society, unlike no other medium.

Amongst the many various differing values that are attributed to sport, below are those which are most relevant to integrated sport, family sport or sport with disabled people.

- **Fairness**

  The value which is most commonly spoken about in sport is fairness. Since sport is played to clear, generally recognised rules, the maintenance of the rules is obvious to all. One is considered as fair when one does not cheat against the opponent; on the contrary one treats him/her as one would want to be treated oneself.

- **Team Spirit; Co-operation**

  In many types of sport, particularly in team sports, one relies on the co-operation of others. Only when everyone is 'pulling in the same direction' will the team be successful. As in the proverbial 'tug-of-war' this is clearly true also in all other team sports such as rowing, soccer, relay races etc. Necessary for this is respect for other team players, with recognition of the part they also play – in other words – good team spirit.

- **Self Achievement**

  Many top sportsmen as well as hobby sportsmen see leisure sports as a possibility to improve their self-achievement. They have the opportunity to visibly develop and improve their capabilities for themselves as well as for others to see. This is so for the physical improvement such as a marathon runner trains to do, or to improve the ability of expression as an ice skater does. Many hobby sportsmen seek personal achievement in their sport, in addition to the fitness component – examples are jogging, cycling, climbing or as a player in a recreational group for soccer, volleyball, tennis and many other types of sport.

- **Determination**

  In sport one can learn to achieve a set goal (i.e., improved performance) by concentrated work and training.

- **Know one's Limits**

  In sport one soon clearly recognises the limits of one's own capability. The recognition of limits and capabilities forms a particularly important step in discovering one's personality – especially for young sportsmen and women.

- **Appreciation of others**

  Part of fairness in sport is the ability to appreciate the performance of the other person – whether partner or opponent. One must be able also to lose.

- **Responsibility**

  Sport offers many opportunities to act responsibly to others; for example:
  - standing by to support in gymnastics
  - act as the older player in support of younger or inexperienced players

- as the team leader
- actively taking part in swimming life-saving exercises
- as exercise leader and coach etc

- **Solidarity**
  Sport offers many people the opportunity to develop the feeling of belonging. One feels 'good' in belonging to such and such a team or such and such a club. The "weaker" ones can also be integrated in this way. Sport therefore offers the chance for the weaker, as well as the disabled, to be integrated and thus show solidarity.

The Motive to Play Sport

Specialist sports literature describes several motives why people play sport, what fascinates them in sport and the reasons why they have turned to sport (c.f. KURZ 1979; LANGE 1977; BRETTSCHNEIDER/BAUR/BRAEUTIGAM 1989 inter alia).

As these motives are well-covered in other sections, at this juncture, I will merely make reference to them: individual development, health and fitness, social contact, holistic development means by motor activity, body awareness, material and spatial experience, fun and joy, playing, performance, excelling, creativity, adventure, risk, learning to confront everyday situations.

Social Structures

In sport we come across differing social structures. These various structures are laid out briefly below, as you will find the games and exercises laid out in these forms in later sections of this book.

- **Individual:**
  Different types of sport can be carried out individually, for oneself or quite alone: examples are running, swimming, cycling, cross-country skiing etc.

- **Partners:**
  For other sports one needs a partner in order that the type of sport or the game can take place: examples are tennis, badminton, tandem bicycle riding etc.

- **Small Groups:**
  Many games and movements are carried out in small groups. Thus naturally for pre-school children's games forming a circle for a game or singing are organised and done in small groups.

- **Teams:**
  The team form determines, by its construction, several types of sport. There are not only team games such as soccer, handball, basketball, volleyball, ice-hockey but also competitions constructed from individual types of sport to make them into team sports such as athletic or swimming relay races, bicycling team competitions etc.

- **Uneven:**
  Some games are designed to be played so that opposing teams do not have the same numbers in them.

- **Free Groups:**
  Unlike team games the free group is not fixed in size, construction, rules etc. Groups can take part in fairs and shows; parachuting, gymnastics, dancing and other group games.

Places to Play in

This section deals briefly with the types of place where "movement, games and sports" can be played.

- **Gymnasium:**
  The gymnasium is the place where most sporting activities take place. It can take the form of a simple hall, a fully equipped gymnasium or a multi-gym room.

- **Sports Field/ Sports Pitch:**
  Many sporting activities are outdoor ones played on a sports pitch.

- **Open Ground:**
  Several games and sporting activities can be carried out away from normal sports facilities i.e., on open ground.

- **Swimming Pool:**
  The swimming pool, whether it be an indoor or an open-air one, is where one can play, either swimming or underwater swimming or alongside the pool edge.

- **The Sea-side/Lake:**
  Water activities are not only suitable for the swimming pool, played at the seaside or in the lake they gain a fresh attractiveness.

- **At Home:**
  Many sporting activities can be played at home, in the living room or on the balcony etc. This does not mean one thinks only of gymnastics or, relaxation exercises or

---

riding the exercise bicycle etc. The home is mostly to be considered where the first movement activities of the child take place – it is where they learn to run and also climb (over the furniture!) and so on.

Target Groups

Sport, and in particular family sport, can be divided up and targeted at differing target groups. In doing this one alters the target according to age and social group structure in the family.

- **Age-Group Structures:**
  Age-groups can be divided into:
  - Babies
  - Infants
  - Children
  - Youths
  - Adults
  - Senior citizens

- **Social Groups:**
  Social groupings can be structured as follows:
  - Women/ men/ mixed groups
  - Schoolchildren/ students/ apprentices/ household staff/ pensioners
  - The unemployed/ foreign citizens or visitors/ fringe groups (i.e., convicts)
  - Disabled or able bodied persons/ integrated groups

Overall Target

The individual should be able to reach his capacity to act, amongst other things, by using sport. Inter alia he can use sport as a possibility to make social contact with others. The overall target for integration in sport is covered in detail in chapter A: II; paragraph 1.4.

11. Sport for the Disabled

"Without his friends, man only lives half a life." (French saying)

The Development of Sport for the Disabled – an Overview

The development of sport for the disabled has moved forward dynamically in two directions in recent years:

• There has been an increase in the number of types and discovery of identified disabilities: Bechterew's disease, endoprotheses, diabetes, osteoporosis, rheumatic illnesses, sports following cancer etc.

• There has been a differentiation in the types of sporting activity available to the disabled. No longer is there only the traditional sports of 'catch' and wheelchair basketball; you can now partake in wheelchair marathons, wheelchair tennis, wheelchair orienteering etc.

If we look back in history, sport for the disabled has not been around very long. In Germany, the first beginnings of so-called disabled sport were seen after World War I when several doctors (HARNACK, KOHLRAUSCH, SCHEDE, WUERTZ, MALLWITZ) encouraged and complemented the medical treatment of the war disabled by the use of specific gymnastic exercises (c.f. KOSEL 1981, 13). Separately to this the German Union for the Deaf ("Deutscher Gehörlosenverband") was founded in 1910. In 1928 the first German club for the blind was founded in Berlin.

After World War 2 sports clubs sprung up throughout the former Federal Republic of Germany on the initiative of young war disabled. Thus, in 1952, the German Sports Union for the War Disabled ("Deutscher Versehrten Sportverband") was formed as the first official sports club for the disabled in Germany.

At the same time sport for the paralysed wheelchair-ridden was developed. This was backed up by the engagement of Sir Ludwig GUTTMANN, an English doctor, who introduced the "Stoke-Mandeville Games" in 1948, and which have now been subsumed into the Olympic Games for the Disabled – the Paralympics.

With the general increase of civil injuries i.e., not war injuries, sufferers also wished to take part in sport. This changed the scene in Germany so that sport for the war disabled became sport for the disabled. As a result the title of the 'German Sports Union for the War Disabled' was changed to the 'German Sports Union for the Disabled' ("Deutscher Behinderten Sportverband" (DBS)) in 1975. Besides the war disabled there is now an increase in injured civilians (e.g., caused by accidents). However there are also children and youths who are born disabled and who find they can experience movement, sports and games in disabled sport.

Nowadays sport for the disabled offers movement, sport and games for physically disabled as well as the mentally disabled, the chronically sick and those threatened with a disability.

Thus, new groups are added to the sphere of disabled sport: cardio-vascular illnesses, coronary diseases, Morbus Bechterew sufferers, multiple sclerosis, spina bifida, cancer victims, diabetics, endoprothesis cases, osteoporosis sufferers, asthmatics etc.

A further impulse comes from those groups and clubs which are giving thought to further integration in sport, besides carrying out sport for and with disabled people. They carry out integrated sport and make use of the experience they gain to confirm that sport is like no other medium as a means for integration.

Target Groups

Sport for the disabled should be open to all those who are disabled [8], that is to say all types – people with impaired vision, physical disabilities and the mentally disabled as well.

As there are so many different kinds of disability conditions, in competitive sport this leads to some problems where performances are to be compared. For example, in swimming, the performance of a paraplegic is not necessarily comparable with that of an arm amputee.

In competitive sport – and also in leisure activities when competing for sports badges – this has lead to the creation of so-called "severity categorisation" to differentiate between competitors in the various disability conditions. For example there are seven categories for the wheelchair-ridden. According to the degree of severity of the disability, one is placed into one or other of the seven categories.

By using such an extreme differentiated system this leads to very few starters appearing for certain event, even in German championships. Categorisation differentiates between the type of disability, degree of severity of the disability and the type of sport itself.

Types of Sport

Limitations in body function or sensory perception result in a corresponding limitation in the type of sport that can be carried out either fully or in part. It would be senseless for the blind to try shooting sports, or paraplegics to attempt climbing.

The types of sport offered must therefore be matched to the limitations of the disabled. Thus we adapt traditional types of sport, or modify and adapt existing sports, or even invent and develop new sports.

An example of the adaptation of existing types of sport is wheelchair basketball played according to the international rules. Thus any able bodied person can sit in a wheelchair and participate with the disabled. An example of modification is sitting volleyball – particularly suitable for leg amputees. On the other hand 'catch', played in the sitting position, is an example of a competitive game developed specifically for leg amputees. Similarly there is goal shooting for the blind by using a ball fitted with a bell inside.

The type of sport that a disabled sportsman takes up does not have to be the same as that which a able bodied sportsman would follow. On the contrary it must match his disability and his interests.

Integrated Sport

Because sport offers itself as an unprecedented excellent sphere of activity for the opportunity to carry out integration, in Germany there has also been a proliferation of newly founded clubs and unions for integrated sport.

In sport one meets each other in a socially defined set of situations e.g., one undertakes to keep to certain generally accepted regulations. This makes it easier for people to get on together in unsure circumstances. This type of getting together gives the opportunity for one to learn about each other in a better way than for example carrying out lengthy discussions.

In this way the disabled and the able bodied can meet in sports and games, get to know each other and dismantle any barriers on both sides, as well as narrow the social distance to disabled people. This is an important first step towards integration.

12. Integration

"When a person dreams alone, it is only a dream.
When many dream the same dream, it is the beginning of a new reality."

(Brazilian saying)

If we consider the circumstances of the disabled in our society, we come to the conclusion that disabled children, youths and families with disabled dependants do not enjoy full participation in social life.

The first chapter contained the argument that the basic principle and aim was that all elements of the population should have the best possible opportunity to take part in society. This stipulated that no one should be excluded or discriminated against. Every individual, every human being should be integrated into society and be a part of that society.

The Term – Integration

What is understood by the term 'integration'? Specialist literature discusses the topic from various directions and with several concepts.

My understanding of integration is in the main the same as the concept of varied integration covered by SPECK in his work "Heilpädagogik" (The Theory of Teaching Medicine) (1988).

SPECK sees integration as the "key word for the principle of social integration of disabled people with other people in naturally and culturally developed areas of common interest – in the learning process, playing together, working together and having fun together, according to their own needs" (SPECK 1988, 288).

SPECK's concept starts with a reciprocal independence of the development of the personality and social integration of the human being, and differentiates between the terms "personal" and "social" integration. At the same time he points out the irreversible dialectical connection of both terms, because being a human being means being considered to others and not just thinking of oneself.

Personal integration means integration on the personal level; the training of the alter ego. "To be oneself or to be at one with oneself, to be able to say yes to oneself and be able to tolerate oneself" is what it is all about (c.f. SPECK 1988, 309). For the disabled person this means that it is necessary to fully accept himself personally as he is.

The integration of individual persons in certain social groups; the taking part in all of society; the adoption of social roles and the assurance of one's place in society is what is understood by the use of the term social integration.

Concurring with FEDJUK (1992, 19), it is true to say that integration in sport is "... that the acceptance of every person (whether disabled or not) and the creation of prerequisites is understood, so that everyone can live as an equal partner regarding his capabilities, requirements, interests and his social commitments in society".

Integration as a Process

The definition of the term 'integration' makes it clear that social integration can only succeed if personal integration happens and vice versa (c.f. SPECK 1988, 16).

This cannot happen by attempting to match the disabled to the norms of society as encouraged by exponents of the "traditional methods of teaching sport to the disabled" (c.f. KOSEL 1981, 20 et seq.). Disabled people do sport amongst themselves; only when they have learned to "behave normally" are they ready for integration.

Another quote tells us that exclusion and non-integration are always preferred as being the easiest and cheapest way forward:

"In my eyes it is preferable to use the method of fitting the disabled into society also by using sport, and this is a very sensible and promising venture. Rather this than to try to make changes towards the creation of a 'society for the disabled' as long as that society is fixed in its thoughts of achievement and harbours misdirected sympathy towards them"

(ASCHER 1991, 44).

However, the social integration of disabled people is to be seen as a process in which not only the social conditions and the attitude of able bodied people have to change, but also the attitude and behaviour of the disabled similarly have to likewise.

I describe this reciprocal influence as a "dialectical process" (c.f. RHEKER 1989a, 123 et seq.). On the one hand there are the existing living conditions with the rigid norms and targets set by our performance-oriented society, and with which the disabled and their sport have to comply without question. Also they have to be changed and modified where they conflict with the development of the human being, the disabled included.

On the other hand it is a question that the individual, again including those who are disabled, is able to develop himself to the full while still remaining attached to society, its possibilities, mechanisms and its abuses.

Thus the individual development of disabled people, and the changed or changing social living conditions, are relative to one another: they affect each other in a dialectical process.

Integration will always be a continuous and progressive process and draws on the principle of experience in concrete situations.

"Integration is ... not a condition, which one can always attain ... integration is a living process, ... integration is to be able to come to terms with one's colleagues in a meaningful way in their lives, to be able to understand one another and to be able to work together. Integration is not achieved once people are not strangers to each other, but only when their mutual esteem rules their behaviour"

(SCHMEICHEL 1983,20).

Only when there is a mutual contact will appreciation for one another succeed. Able bodied people learn, by coming directly into contact, not to value a person by his appearance or his cognitive capabilities, but rather to develop an acceptance as well as an understanding and a sensitivity towards that other person. Behavioural insecurities and negative attitudes can be broken down in this way.

Furthermore this makes it possible not always to stigmatise a disability but to live and learn that person's personality in all its possible forms.

In the common process of coming together, everyone tries to understand oneself, and the next man as well, in order to learn a way of living together on these principles. In this all elements of the personality must be considered.

Attitudes are either gained or modified by the process of communication and interaction. Direct contact between the disabled and able bodied is the starting point for a change of attitude towards disabled people and their families. It is also the way to close the social distance and learn how to view the disabled as individuals, who besides many other peculiarities have a particular disability.

Thus people who enjoy good contact with disabled people, have hardly any prejudices and retain a positive attitude.

"People, who have good contacts with the disabled, will show a better attitude towards them than those who do not... The more often contact with the disabled takes place, the more positive is the attitude of those involved"
(CLOERKES 1982, 563).

Because the formation of attitude occurs between about the age three or four to eight years old (c.f. inter alia DREYER 1981, 58), efforts to integrate should begin as early as possible.

In summary it can be said that the road to integration is not by having sympathy, but by filling the information gap and getting rid of prejudices so that more possibilities for interactivity between the disabled and able bodied are realised. The deciding factor will be how often and to what intensity such meetings together take place.

The Idea of Normalisation

One central theme in the social integration of disabled persons is the one that BENGT NIRJE developed in Scandinavia as a principle of normalisation for the mentally disabled target group. In this it is a question of "assisting the mentally disabled to lead a life that is structured as normally as possible" (NIRJE 1974, 34).

Transposed into the whole span of the disabled, this means that the same conditions of life and the same rights are afforded to the disabled as they are to the able bodied. As a result, normalisation is a social-political principle of equality that is bound firmly to the basic rights of each citizen.

"Normalisation means the acceptance of people, together with their disabilities, into 'normal' society, with the same rights, the same responsibility and the same opportunities as afforded to others."

(NIRJE/PERRIN 1986, 8).

The acceptance of 'being disabled' as normality is a basic condition for the social integration of the disabled.

Integration is to be seen as a process of reciprocal adaptation in which all involved learn from one another – not only the disabled learning from the able bodied, but also vice versa.

Integration in Sport

There is a general consensus in our society regarding the necessity of integrative measures. Because of its varied interactive and communicative properties, sport is considered to be a very suitable scenario for joint activities between disabled and able bodied.

For a long time, the DSB has been promoting the target "sport for everyone" and wants to " ... involve our country's (Germany) citizens who are crowding the doors of our gymnastics and sports clubs" (Kultusministerium (German Ministry of Culture) NRW 1982, 8). This target is aimed at the area of mass sports above all. It also concerns " ... the business of effectively improving the prerequisites for a more intensive incorporation of socially disadvantaged groups in our society" ((Kultusministerium (German Ministry of Culture) 1982, 8).

However, not every type of sport is suitable for adaptation and integration of disabled people. WURZEL (1991) emphasised that sport did not represent a particularly suitable arena for thoughts on integration. Indeed the opposite was the case because the inherent considerations of high performance in sport worked contrarily against it. Moreover, HAEP (1987) draws attention to the fact that the characteristic of a disability compared with not having one is shown up particularly in sport and thus made any thoughts of integration difficult.

Against the backdrop of these critical objections it seems necessary to check out what problems exist with the ascribed characteristics of sport in dealing with integration. They must not be accepted simply as obvious.

The circumstances where sport does contribute to integration must be examined. This leads to describing the various ways of how integration in sport is considered. For example integration can be described as a formal term meaning the "outward appearance" of the meeting up of various groups of people for differing circumstances e.g., for a short period, for a games festival, or as a heterogeneous group, or as a sports club grouping.

These heterogeneous groups (or the heterogeneity of a group) say something about the organisational association within the group but nothing about the intensity of relationships between the group members. Integration, viewed from the perspective of content, is best described as a process and an aim.

In order to achieve the target of "integration", a process must be initiated which brings about changes in attitude. The naive supposition that it is only to do with contact alone must be replaced by a series of positive conditions in order to improve the relationships between the disabled and the able bodied: intensity of the relationship, personal engagement, a basically positive attitude, gregariousness, a will to make contact and the following of joint aims and tasks inter alia (see CLOERKES 1979 and compare 'the horizontal and vertical dimensions of integration', chapter II.1.2 and RHEKER 1996).

So that such a process of social co-existence can be made effective, above all in the subject of sport, possibilities for interactivity and communication between the disabled and the able bodied are required.

Because of a number of factors such as the differing levels of expertise and experience, individual mobility, and above all, differing inclinations, demands and interests of the participants, integration in sport must be represented by a broad-based variety of sporting opportunities.

The arena of sport offers fringe groups (foreigners, convicts, addicts, asylum seekers, the unemployed, the old aged and also the disabled) the possibility to integrate socially in society.

Sport for the disabled in an integrated environment has, up to now, been seen more as a peripheral activity. Only a few model groups and clubs have attempted to turn the thoughts on integration into deeds.

In many sports clubs for the disabled, however, participants are all too often kept in "like" groups i.e., separate groups for leg amputees, cerebral palsy sufferers, spina bifida victims etc. Unfortunately many doctors recommend parents of disabled children to place them only in these segregated groupings, claiming that they will be treated equally according to their specific disability. Some doctors and therapists see disabled children as "ailing", and who can only be "normalised" by such a therapy.

Disabled people are not only defined and categorised by virtue of their disability. They also have individual personalities and many different characteristics that can be better handled and treated in integrated groupings.

Summarising – integration in sport is, in the first instance, oriented to leisure activities between disabled and able bodied people. Its primary aim is devoted to the optimum development of the disabled as well as their social integration. By using the experiences gained from the many opportunities of communication and interactivity offered by sport, social contact through sport can be built up free of the stigma of being disabled. How this can be achieved in practice has been shown, in Germany, by numerous models and the initiatives of organisations.

---

1   Article 1, Paragraph 1 of the Federal German Constitution 23rd May 1949; c.f. also JAKOBI,P./ROESCH, H-E., 1982.
2   Explanation: Norm is, exactly like handicap, to be seen in its social and historic relevance and is defined as the valid behavioural manner or its rules; as per the expected manners between people and by people in the environment (c.f. BELLEBAUM 1974, 50 et seq.).
3   Explanation: Attribution with a negative and incriminating characteristic, negative regarding non-relevance, not filling role expectations.
4   In this context the behavioural pattern regarding disabled people refers to e.g., the Third Reich, which carried out mass murders of disabled people.
5   Project "Movement, Games and Sports with Disabled Children" Ministry of Culture North Rhine Westphalia/ 'Behinderten-Sportverband' (Sports Union for the Disabled)/Paderborn University (BRETTSCHNEIDER/RHEKER) – results of a research report – as yet unpublished figures.
6   Quoting SPECK (1980, 111).
7   Answers range from a scale of 5 equals "totally applicable" to 1 equals "not at all applicable".
8   See DBS 1985.

II. Models for Integration in Sport

"Rather light a candle than curse the darkness" (Chinese saying).

The following passages deal with two integrated sports groups in Germany which have placed joint co-operation in movement, games and sports for disabled children and youths together with able bodied adolescents as a central aim.

Since these groups are trying out and working to realise different methods, they can be considered as distinct varied models of integration. As 'models' they do not wish to, nor indeed should be seen as unique exceptions. On the contrary they want to demonstrate a method of how co-existence between young disabled and able bodied can be turned into normality.

One of the groups is an integrated family sports group for disabled and able bodied children, which consciously did not form its own disabled sport club but formed an association with an existing "normal" sports club – TuRa Elsen.

A further group – the Paderborn Ahorn-Panthers – is described, which specialises on children's wheelchair sports and belongs to a parent club for integrated disabled sport. The principle of joint co-existence for disabled and able bodied people is anchored firmly in the charter of the parent club.

1. Integration in Family Sport

"The best thing is that suddenly one forgets that your children are disabled. Everything is so normal. [....] Everyone treats the disabled as if they were normal beings".[9]

1.1 Creation and Development

The idea to form a family sports group for disabled children and youths came about during some of the family leisure activity periods. Planning and realisation was carried out in conjunction with the university and the Hermann-Schmidt-School – a school for the mentally disabled in Schloss-Neuhaus, Paderborn during 1981 and 1982.

Aim of the leisure activity periods was originally, and still is, to experience and share opportunities and possibilities for their creation and design, to discuss problems and to find solutions to special topics and themes such as; living with disabled people, the society's attitude to disabled people etc.

In the leisure periods the subject of movement, games and sports was considered so important that the desire to initiate and include a regular opportunity of sport sessions for families with disabled children was expressed.

First of all, in June 1982, we organised activity sessions for family sport in conjunction with the "Verein zur Hilfe Geistigbehinderter (lit., Club to Help the Mentally Disabled)" in the gymnasium of the Hermann-Schmidt School. Then, after that, at the end of 1982, we formed our own section as a part of, and in association with, the large Paderborn Sports Club TuRa Elsen (2,500 members). At the same time we transferred the afternoon exercise sessions to the large gymnasium of Paderborn University/Polytechnic which afforded the growing group more opportunities. In the meanwhile the group had swelled from the twelve families involved during the foundation period to more than fifty.

Between 60 to 100 people come together between 1500-1700 hours on every second and fourth Saturday in the month in the University gymnasium to play, sing, dance and partake in sport together. In addition there are many other joint activities for the family sports groups.

As an exemplary model of an integrated sports group, in 1990 the 'Paderborn Family Sports Group' was awarded the "Fach-Sport-Behindertenpreis (lit., Disabled Sports Branch Prize)" worth 5,000 DM.

Picture 2: Michael Gross hands over the "Fach-Sport-Behindertenpreis 1990" award to Uwe Rheker

1.2   Concept

Integrated family sport developed from the joint experiences and participation in sport by families with disabled children together with families of able bodied children, and its conception was carried out with this in mind. The Paderborn model of integrated sport should not be seen as unique, nor does it wish to be seen as exceptional. On the contrary it should allow co-existence between disabled and able bodied to be experienced as a 'slice' of normality.

The theory of differentiated integration, as described above, has its roots in the experiences of integrated sport. Critical reflection on those experiences leads to the theory, which remains continually reliant on accepted practice and at the same time seeks to strive towards social changes for this. We find a similar viewpoint in liberation theology which for example in Brazil, dealt first of all with the accepted practice used in dealing with the suppressed and for those 'cast out' and then developed into a theory "Theology of Liberation" (c.f. GUTIERREZ 1982). That is why we find the principles of this theory here as there – again in accepted practice.

Differentiated integration – which is understood as a reciprocal dependence on the development of the personality and social environment – is given a chance of being realised through the accepted practice of family sport for disabled and able bodied.

In the "Paderborn model of integrated family sports" there is, in addition to activities for the whole family, an opportunity for differentiated sport for the various large heterogeneous target groups. In this way each person gains room for individual development (personal integration).

The various target groups are able to realise their own wishes and ideas regarding movement, games and sport:
- Parents can follow their own activities for a part of the session without having to watch out for their children all the time.
- Disabled children, and the younger able bodied children, can concentrate on their motor and social behavioural demands.
- Youngsters have space in a part of the gymnasium where they can really romp freely.
- Pre-school children have the opportunity to learn the special games for this target group in the gymnastics section of the hall.

With the whole family involved this also allows social integration – the binding together of individuals into social groups. Family sport between disabled and able bodied people allows social integration on different levels by virtue of the fact that quite different target groups are partaking in joint sport together: disabled and able bodied, men and women, the old and the young, people with different types of disability, serious athletes and recreational sportsmen, as well as people with differing expectations from their participation in sport.

• Horizontal and Vertical Dimensions of Integration

Integration in one of these integrative family sports groups can be achieved by **different dimensions and degrees.** The fact is that quite different target groups converge to take part in joint sport. However, merely the fact that different groups meet up together cannot be seen alone as integration in the true sense of the word.

The outward, formal side of integration can be also taken as the **horizontal dimension** of integration, which gives the opportunity for heterogeneous groups to meet up.

The **vertical dimension** of integration, which can also be called the intensifying dimension of integration, manifests itself by the quality of the co-existence – by the way members of the group get along with one another.

The frankness exercised amongst the members within the group is an important condition for a positive basic attitude between all involved. This permits each to accept the other as a person, unshackled by one's capability to perform or achieve, one's appearance, one's social status and any possible disability.

The pursuit of joint aims and tasks belongs equally to the integration process that might lead on from the horizontal dimension. Thus the aims and tasks can reach beyond just sport and bring emphasis to the social co-existence and responsibility for all group members.

Personal engagement and the intensity of relationships with one another lends further aid, so that integration as a process can happen and can lead to changes of attitude and positive attitudes. As a result the vertical dimension of integration is promoted.

The fact that, in the TuRa Elsen, conditions for achievement of integration in the family sports group are so well-advanced, also in the vertical dimension, is demonstrated admirably by the open and caring atmosphere exuded by the group. New families and visitors are integrated at once, so much so that they immediately feel they belong. The intensity of relationships can be felt in family leisure periods in which families with their disabled and able bodied children spend a week or perhaps a long week-end together. This is also present in the regular mother or parent meetings where mutual experiences are exchanged and problems discussed.

Personal engagement in one's own sports group is not only a factor for the exercise leaders and assistants. It is also very much something which the parents take part in. This occurs in the normal sports afternoons, and is particularly noticeable in the preparation and execution of events which are planned in addition to the regular family sports sessions – family leisure periods, club fêtes, sports festivals, family prayer sessions, hikes.

The different levels on which integration in such family sports groups can be achieved, are not on a par with each other. On the contrary they are weighted in many differing degrees. There is a special importance attached to the level on which one arrives at the integration between disabled and able bodied people. On each of these levels integration is a question of specifics i.e., to achieve integration in the vertical dimension.

• Integration and the Generation Gap
Whenever children and youths of different ages play together or partake in sport, they have to show consideration for differing demands and expectations. Even more understanding, tolerance and adjustment is expected if the age gap stretches over several generations. In the family sports group there are often up to three generations taking part in joint sport – from the infant of one or two years old to the sprightly 'grandma' who has come with her disabled grandchild.

By virtue of the open coming and going together in the group, there will often be spontaneous contact between the different age-groups. In playing together, the parents will join in with their disabled and able bodied children, and younger children will seek contact with older children.

From these loose initial contacts firm friendship builds up often leading to the expression of an invitation to birthday parties, and an exchange of letters in the interval between the family sports meetings.

In particular games, involving communication and interactivity these, promote the coming together of quite different age-groups. Given the positive basic attitude of the members of a sports group amongst themselves, relationships will be strengthened through the joint exercises undertaken.

• Integration Case: The Sexes
Co-education of boys and girls does not specifically have to be a separate subject for discussion when considering sport for the family. It is obvious that in family sport, boys and girls and men and women will join together.

• Integration Case: The Level of Expectation, Motives and Degree of Skill
Traditional sports clubs have to offer people who take up sport with different expectations and motives a variety of movement, games and sports e.g., recreational sports, therapeutic sports, competitive sports, leisure sports or spinal exercises, swimming, soccer, volleyball etc. To this the often various degree of skill amongst recreational players, amateurs, local league players, top division, 1st team players through to the professionals, must be added.

By contrast, integrated sport brings together the different expectations, motives and degrees of skill. In family sport all sorts of people come together to participate – ex-competitive sportsmen and women, leisure and recreational players and some who just 'dabble' in sports, infants, youths and adults – all people who have quite different demands, orientation and capabilities.

Joint activity in the games and sports calls for mutual understanding and respect and promotes these qualities. One learns about the capabilities and needs of the other person and how to accept them. Very often parents learn that their offspring can do a lot more than they gave them credit for previously.

Moreover intensive contact is a product of any joint activity. It begins with mutual discussion before and after the exercise periods and leads on to regular rendezvous e.g., ranging from discussion groups for mothers through to flute-playing groups etc.

In the Paderborn model four different groups[10] have been formed for integrated family sports sessions, so that justice can be done to all the different participants' expectations.

Subsequently each person is given room for individual development. This also gives everyone the possibility to join in the group with one's own individual capability and thus be well-accepted.

• Integration Case: The Differing Types of Disability
While several sports clubs for the disabled offer various activities for different types of disability in segregated groups, integrated sport can easily bring together people with different types of disability.

Originally the family sports group was formed following the initiative of parents with mentally disabled children. From the beginning, however, no other disabled persons were excluded and all-comers were deliberately incorporated. The sports group is open to all types of disability. Families meet up for joint afternoon activities with mentally disabled, physically disabled, people with several disabilities and the partially deaf.

Just how intensive integration is achieved in this case will be seen much clearer in the next case.

• Integration Case: The Disabled and Able Bodied

Only a very few normal sports clubs are open to disabled people. Almost as few clubs for the disabled integrate the able bodied. Integrated sport, on the other hand, couples both the disabled and the able bodied.

Family sports groups are planned to be open i.e., not only can families with disabled members, but also their friends as well as families with able bodied children, participate in the group from the very beginning. In this way joint games and sports between disabled and able bodied people become a natural thing. Opportunity is created for meetings free of any prejudices. People learn to accept each other and break down any existing prejudices. For some parents and children it serves as a small step to escape isolation.

The normalisation and understanding for families with disabled and able bodied children can be seen in the following observations.

Several parents of disabled children have learnt that many of the problems they experience with their children, and specific questions regarding disabilities, can be taken up and placed in context. They also learn that many of the problems that parents have with able bodied children are common to those that they themselves have to deal with.

Just how joint activity between disabled and able bodied children has become a natural thing is born out by remarks made by visitors and activity assistants. It is quite clear that by virtue of the openness of the group, the children are so well-integrated that they hardly appear to be 'disabled'. Representative of the parents' view, the following was said during a television interview:

> "The best thing is that suddenly one forgets that your children are disabled. Everything is so normal. [....] Everyone treats the disabled as if they were normal beings."

Integration Case: Clubs

In our case no separate disabled sports club was formed. This was done in order to give the process of integration a broad basis and not limit it to the family sports group. The integrated family sports group joined forces with an existing gymnastics and sports club on the outskirts of Paderborn with the name of TuRa Elsen.

In this way it created many possibilities to organise things together with other sections of the club while, of course, the disabled and able bodied still remained integrated. The family sports group takes part in games such as the "It's a Knockout" type, in sports festivals for youngsters or in club anniversaries, and simply these now have become a standard part of them. The group also takes disabled and able bodied children on youth outings.

These efforts at integration came over particularly well at various youth camps in the Sauerland region (an area south of Paderborn). In addition the mothers' group is well-integrated in the whole of the club. As well as other things they take part every year in the Ladies Carnival and give an exhibition of self-choreographed dancing.

1.3   Sport in Action
Besides sport for the whole family, the 'Paderborn Family Sports Group' has targets for other various groups. In addition there are project periods and further activities such as swimming, hiking, sports festivals etc.

Sport for the Whole Family
With the motto of the DSB "sport for everyone" in mind, the main thrust is all about getting the family together to be active, play games and partake in sport. Each sports session begins and ends with joint singing, playing and dancing.

Besides dancing and gymnastics there are particularly suitable games available from the inexhaustible list of 'little basic games':

Picture 3: Games with the parachute, painted by ourselves, are particularly suitable for group movements and actions in the sports group.

- Games with party balloons and balls made of paper machée
- Running and catching games such as catch; chain catch, chain catch in twos or threes, touch rugby and games like for example 'magic mouse.'
- Small ball games like 'Hunter ball' in its various forms, 'Völker-Ball', ball over the rope.
- Movement exercises to music like the 'Molecular game'.
- Singing games and other little games and dancing.
- Trampolines and the giant bouncy air beds are particularly popular equipment as well as others often used such as the parachute, pedal-vehicles and other psychomotor exercise equipment.

Different Ways of Organising Sport

In order to accommodate heterogeneous different target groups better, and to serve their expectations well, the group is split into four single sections after the first part of a joint session.

With more than 90 people taking part this is necessary. The space afforded in the large gymnasium with its multi-gym room makes this also possible. Doing so also allows for differing age-groups and target groups to be formed.

• Sports for the Parents

In one section of the gymnasium the parents can do something for their own fitness and health, enabling them to develop their sporting wishes without the "stress" of having the children about. This takes the form of badminton, indoor-hockey, volleyball or dancing, relaxing exercises, spinal exercises etc.

• Specific Sports for the Disabled and Able Bodied Younger Children

In another part of the gymnasium, specific sports for the disabled children and the younger able bodied children is carried out. Because there is a large number of exercise leaders and assistants, special attention is available to take care of the disabled and this is very necessary.

In addition to the main aim of getting the disabled and able bodied children to learn to play together and take part in sport, the following aims are also realised:

> • Encouragement of motor activity
> • Discovering body movements
> • Learning about equipment
> • Social experiences.

For this activity, trampoline and gymnastics are used alternately.

- **Specific Sports for Older Able Bodied Brothers and Sisters and Disabled Youths**

Similarly to the parents, the aim with this group is to allow the participants to develop their sporting wishes and to give them the opportunity to satisfy their movement activities. Besides taking the social aspects of this target group into consideration, younger and disabled children must be given the space to be able to follow up their own expectations for sport.

Individual wishes for the content of the sports programme are put in first place. To this end activities such as the high jump, skate boarding, table tennis or trampoline inter alia are selected. Very often strenuous activities such as indoor-hockey, soccer or badminton are also played in this group and the fathers often join in.

• **The Crawler Group**

Because in the last few years many parents with children in the pre-school age have turned up, a so-called "crawler" group has been established. This meets in the multi-gym room to carry out circular holding hands ("Ring-a-ring a roses") and singing games as well as other games dealing with experiencing the body, equipment and social aims[11] .

At the end of each session everyone meets up together again. Family sport always ends with a joint session of singing, playing and dancing.

Project Sessions

Several times each year the whole of the family sports group works on a special theme. In these project sessions the whole of the sports afternoon is devoted to a motto such as circus, sports studio, carnival, a winter or pre-winter theme, pirates island etc.

For these the gymnasium is decked out appropriately e.g., as a circus tent or a sports studio etc. Following a joint introduction, workshops are formed in which the individual programme points in the project theme are put together. Everyone can input to the work group with his own ideas and suggestions. In this way a colourful and varied programme is developed, which everyone has contributed towards to make it a success.

A joint finale rounds off the project. In general it can be said that project sessions are often one of the highpoints in the activities of the family sports group.

Further Activities in the Family Sports Group

Besides the regular sports afternoons in the gymnasium there are many events and meetings which bring the group together in more general areas other than sports. This gives room, over and above other things, to get to know each other better and to exchange views. Problems and one's own experiences can be discussed and new ideas worked up for joint activity sessions. The following additional activities are on offer:

- At least once a year the whole group takes part in a **leisure weekend** in an educational institute with lots of sporting possibilities. This enables the group to bond together and allows the newly joined members an opportunity to mould in better with the group. These leisure periods often take the form of a particular theme e.g., autonomous training for disabled children.
- Furthermore, we hold a **games fête** once a year with the giant air bed as the middle point and also invite other disabled sports groups and children's groups to take part. The closing session of such an event is a barbecue party when social and communicational aspects come to the fore.
- Occasionally we organise a joint **walk** with open air games and a barbecue party to round it off.
- Besides all of this, joint games and **swimming** in public baths belong as a firm part of the family sports group schedule. We have had some happy experiences in this when, in particular during playtime, other children have spontaneously joined in. This has brought with it an open opportunity for activities with the disabled and able bodied children without insurmountable barriers existing.
- In the same way joint actions are set up for disabled and able bodied people to receive **sports medals**. Non-members can also take part so that even more areas are available for mutual activity between disabled and able bodied people and thereby prejudices and attitudes can be changed.
- The mother's meeting, providing a regular **exchange of experiences**, has become a firm part of the programme. From this even an independent "flautist group" has been formed.
- **Joint activities** with the TuRa Club Elsen. Here is a selection from the full programme of possibilities that can be carried out together with the main club, and in particular with the gymnastics section: youth outings, youth sports fêtes, youth camps, carnivals, joint appearances at anniversaries, gymnastics festivals, gymnasium openings etc., Christmas festivals, sports and gymnastics medal prize giving and so on and so forth.

Integrated family sport along the lines of the Paderborn model encourages integration on several levels, and at the same time allows the joint working together of disabled and able bodied to become a reality.

It is therefore an aim, moving on from the phase of the example of family sport with disabled people, that joint sports and games and the participation of disabled and able bodied people in sport will become normal.

1.4   Setting the Aims
"Wherever two people put their arms around each other, a circle is formed"
(HEBBEL 1984, 94).

The following list of objectives for family sports is based on several statements concerning the interpretation and didactic results of sport instruction (c.f. inter alia KURZ 1977, 1979; LANGE 1977; EHNI 1985).

For use in family sports, the aims have been expressed loosely. First of all the overarching aim can be defined as:

The individual, whether he be disabled or able bodied, should be able to achieve and develop his capacity to act.

When actually carrying out family sports, the following objectives should be achieved:
• Joint activities for the whole family.
• Give the opportunity for joint activities between families with disabled children and families with able bodied children.
• Allow the individual development of each person.
• Improve one's own health and fitness.
• Afford and intensify social contact.
• Encourage holistic development using motor activity.
• Family sport should permit one to learn about one's body and generally about oneself.
• Family sport should permit one to learn about equipment and the environment.
• Family sport should be fun and bring joy for all.
• Be able to play.
• Improve performance ability (of the body).
• Be able to produce movement activity and develop creativity.
• Discover the perspectives of adventure and risk.
• Prepare one for everyday situations.

The first two objectives are of paramount importance.

• Joint Activities for the whole Family

"... you'll see, if one gets down to it together,
you can pull up even the biggest turnip out of the ground."

(KJG Song Book 1 1985, 78 et seq.)

The family sports group carries out games and sport together allowing all members of the family to get to know each other better, and by using joint experiences come closer together. It also allows the whole family to bond together and have a better understanding.

Parents often experience that their children can do more than they would have given credit to up to now. Similarly the children learn about their parents, experiencing them in a different set of situations, with different roles, and seeing them in a different light.

Joint sport between parents, children and youths teaches one to accept the different abilities and demands of the other person, to understand them and to take them into account.

• Give the Opportunity for Joint Activities between Families with Disabled Children and Families with Able Bodied Children

Statement by a mother on the integration of this group:
"Somehow it is a group that simply is generally integrated. It is where anyone can be integrated, whether they are disabled or not, or a foreigner, or perhaps just a little noticeable in their behaviour. This does not matter at all in this group"

(KREIß 1994, 122).

If family sport for families with disabled children and families with able bodied children is on offer from the very beginning, this affords a grouping free of prejudices, allowing a mutual acceptance and the diminution of any existing prejudices on both sides.

Using games and sports joint activities between disabled and able bodied people can become something quite normal. Particularly children together learn to accept the other as a person very quickly. They learn to view disabled people as personalities with this or that capability, and not to view them primarily according to the stigmatisation of the disability itself.

For parents, the family sports group provides an opportunity to make and create contacts.

• Allow the Individual Development of each Person
Besides the joint activities of the whole family, it is also important that the individual can contribute to the sport and activities and realise his expectations.

In family sport, one is supposedly dealing with very different target groups. We have retired competitive sportsmen and others who have never taken part in sport at all. We have little children at the crawling stage, and youths with specific expectations of what constitutes a sports afternoon. We have disabled children with varying different disabilities and able bodied children. The furtherance of the whole complex of the personality, regarding the aim and incentives of motor activity, is particularly important for the younger children and the disabled children.

Because family sport can encompass sometimes three generations (children, parents and grandparents), one must take into account the different expectations each has in games and sports.

Only when it has been successful in meeting the expectations and allowing each to "have his say" in at least one part of the sports session, will the versatility of family sport come into its own. If this is not achieved then a part of the group will gradually drop out. Such a case can be avoided by ensuring that there is at least a wide variety of things on offer in one part of the sports session.

• Improving one's own Health and Fitness
Many who join a sports club or play sport for leisure, do this from the perspective of doing something for their health and fitness. This means very often that they do it to create a balance in everyday burdens or to counter the single-sided demands of a profession.

The content of family sport must be organised therefore with this aim in mind, and an appropriate accent placed on the way things are put together. Thus, intensive activities and games must be included in each sports session, which above all stimulate the cardio-respiratory circulation. Also the fun and pleasure, which ensue from these games and sports, have a positive effect on the well-being and health of one's whole personality.

However a part of health are the terms posture, strengthening of the posture and relaxation. These aims can be achieved by gymnastic exercises which set a corresponding emphasis and include exercises such as tension and relaxation exercises and spinal cord exercises, particularly for the parent target group or children at risk to posture defects.

Included in the objective for health and fitness there is a broad spectrum of terms to be taken into account – as defined also by the World Health Organisation (WHO). The psychological side, and with it the emotional state of well-being, fun, pleasure, relaxation etc., complement the organic physical dimension of cardio-respiratory circulation and muscle exercises and take into account the social situation.

• **Afford and Intensify Social Contact**

"There is always a lot spoken about a family with a mentally disabled child.
Frequently it is not seen in a good light"

(VON BRACKEN 1976, 117).

Besides the health aspects, another equally important reason to join a sports group is the desire for social contact, socialising and company. This aim plays an important role, particularly for families with disabled children. These families are often more isolated than others.

The aim of social contact can be achieved on different levels in an integrated family sports group:
– Joint participation in sports and games can ameliorate the relationships within the family. The parents learn about their children from another, perhaps also new, side and discover new capabilities in themselves. Also relationships between able bodied brothers and sisters and their disabled ones can be improved by doing things together during leisure activities.
– In family sport with disabled people, contacts can be made with families who have the same problems. Parents often discover that their problems are not that big as they appear when they see them on their own.
– Furthermore, integrated family sport gives the opportunity for social contact between families with disabled children and families with able bodied children. The contact often continues outside the sport sessions. Contact is deepened by joint leisure participation and other activities which are on offer besides the joint sports sessions. We have experienced that parents with disabled children are able to place their problems regarding the specific disability into context when they find out that other families with able bodied children have the same, if not similar, problems.
– When an integrated family sports group is intertwined in a "normal sports group" there are many more possibilities for social contact and contact with other sections of the club. This allows for joint participation and more intensive contact with people from other parts of the club – festivals, carnivals, games and sports events, outings and camps.

About the Concept

In the children's wheelchair group there are children with various disabilities (inter alia spina bifida, walking disabled and mentally disabled children) together with able bodied children doing games and sports. So that this all happens under the same conditions, the children who are not normally dependent on the wheelchair use this equipment for sporting activities.

The sports wheelchair is for most children such an attractive sports equipment and plaything that sometimes there not are enough of them to go round, although, there are about 20 wheelchairs, available. A further advantage, speaking for the joint usage of the sports wheelchair is that first of all the able bodied children can learn how to operate the wheelchair from the disabled children. This has shown that the necessary learning process also really works mutually and is no one-way road on which the disabled people have to adapt themselves as far as possible to the ways of the able bodied.

The group meets regularly on Wednesday afternoons for 1 1/2 hours in the Ahorn Sports Park. This large sports centre has open hall segments i.e., there are no dividing walls between the five playing surfaces. They are merely divided by using nets. Surrounding the playing surfaces there is a 200 m running track with a view into the inside area. Thus the children are not in an isolated area but rather other activities are going on all around.

Doing sport together gives the opportunity for additional contacts and meeting up of people of the same age. Many able bodied children, who have called by just to have a look at what is going on, would also like to join in or have already done so in the past.

The opportunity for the children's group to do sport with others presents itself as another form of integration. Indeed sometimes the children are often distracted by activities in the other playing areas, but the realisation that they are able to practice their own sport together naturally with other sportsmen on an equal basis, mitigates against this disadvantage.

The group is controlled by two exercise leaders and a group assistant. The children are able to bring their own ideas and interests into the sport. After the introductory discussion the programme for the session is put together. Besides games to further wheelchair skills (catching games, obstacle courses inter alia), the games that stand out from the others are those whose objective it is to include joint activities (games with the parachute, games and movement to music, small ball games such as 'Hunter ball', group ball games, or basketball) between disabled and able bodied children – or said another way – children coming together who have different requirements. On top of this, a concentrated but relaxed series of wheelchair gymnastics forms a part of every session.

Characteristic of sport for the disabled is the dependence of the disabled children on transport to bring them to the sessions. In the children's group it is the parents who regularly bring their children to sport and fetch them afterwards. They do not take part in the sport themselves so that the children do not feel that they are being watched by them. The 1 1/2 hour session is therefore used by them to form a parent's circle. It takes place at the same location (in the Ahorn Sports Park Café) and gives those taking part the opportunity to exchange information and have a "natter". These meetings have developed into friendships which have proved to be very beneficial to the atmosphere in the group. By the parents taking part, this has been an additional successful factor in binding the children long-term into the group.

Besides the regular sports sessions, the sections of the Integrated Paderborn Ahorn-Panthers Club take part in various events which brings together disabled and able bodied people from other regions: wheelchair orienteering, integrated wheelchair basketball tournaments, amateur marathon-type running, which is organised so that both disabled and able bodied people can take part together, leisure weekends (with the whole family), boat trips, mini-golf, hiking and joint outings and holiday camps (e.g., with the Scouts).

Picture 4: Friendships also bloom during an integrated Scout's camp with the children's wheelchair sports group.

All these types of activity (from the preparation phase of the organisation through to the evaluation) present a number of opportunities for disabled and able bodied persons to meet. It allows situations to arise where we get to know how the disabled live. This leads (or can lead) to the ability, for the disabled as well as the able bodied, to be able to change attitudes towards one another.

9   Interview with Mrs B. in a television interview about the family sports group for disabled in TuRa Elsen. TV Programme "Aktuelle Stunde", WDR, 19th June 1990.
10 Compare Integrated Family Sport.
11 Compare Games-Data Bank.
12 From the speech of the school representative Dirk STRUCK (disabled and wheelchair ridden) on the occasion of the opening of the gymnasium of the Westphalian School for the Disabled in Paderborn on 16.3.1991.
13 Interview with Mrs K. (1990) in connection with the project "Movement, Games and Sports with Disabled Children and Youths" Paderborn University in conjunction with the Ministry of Culture North Rhine Westphalia and the 'Behinderten-Sportverband NRW' (Sports Union for the Disabled).
14 BRETTSCHNEIDER, W-D/RHEKER, U: "Movement, Games and Sports with Disabled Children and Youths" Project of the Ministry of Culture North Rhine Westphalia/'Behinderten-Sportverband' (Sports Union for the Disabled), and Paderborn University, 1989-92.
15 Interview with Mrs K (1990) in connection with the project "Movement, Games and Sports with Disabled Children and Youths" Paderborn University in conjunction with the Ministry of Culture North Rhine Westphalia and the 'Behinderten-Sportverband NRW' (Sports Union for the Disabled).

B. INTEGRATION IN SPORT

This chapter, illustrating the practice of integrated sport, is divided into five sections. The first four are devoted to integrated family sport and the fifth section describes integrated wheelchair sport.

The games included in the individual sections are not necessarily exclusively only meant for these sections. Rather they can be used in various situations and for differing objectives and in other types of sporting connections (see Games - Data Bank).

In the first section there is a description of the games and exercise forms which have the theme of games and sport for the whole family – in Paderborn integrated family sport session begins and ends with joint games. The second section shows the possibilities for differentiated sport for the various target groups in family sport:

1. Disabled and young able bodied children
2. Parents
3. Disabled youths and able bodied older children
4. Crawler groups

Along the theme of projects and games, the third section introduces theme games such as circus, gymnastics, carnivals etc. The fourth section, concerning family sports, is devoted to activities outside the gymnasium such as leisure sessions for the family, hiking, swimming and games festivals. In the last section there is a description of games and exercise forms for integrated wheelchair sport.

In order to avoid repetition games are only shown once, although they could be included in many of the other sections. Many of the games described are used in quite different integrated groups and can be applied to many other sporting situations e.g., a large number of the games are aquatic and are suitable for any type of beginner's swimming exercises, irrespective of disability or not, and equally for leisure swimming groups or for loosening-up gymnastic exercises and other aquatic exercises.

Many of these games can also serve to give a stimulus for sport with other target groups: children's sports groups, mother and child groups, leisure and health sports groups such as coronary sufferer's sport, sport for diabetics, osteoporosis groups, overweight persons groups, psychomotor groups and a whole host more.

In order to cope with the complexity of the games, the project "Movement, Games and Sports for Disabled Children and Youths" they were compiled into a games' data-bank together with other games, using a system of different categories. This makes it possible to look up games according to location, social form, organisation, material/equipment, activity, intention, experience and suitability for the wheelchair ridden (see diagram 1). Each of these categories contains criteria which are of central importance for each game.

Diagram 1: Games Data-Bank

GAMES DATA-BANK

NAME: _-_-_-_-_-_-_-_

LOCATION:		SOCIAL FORM:		ORGANISATION:		MAT/EQPT:	
GYM	0	INDIVIDUAL	0	CIRCLE	0	BALL	0
FIELD	0	PARTNER	0	RELAY	0	GYM EQPT	0
OPEN GROUND	0	SMALL GROUP	0	PITCH	0	PSYCHOMOTOR	0
WATER	0	TEAM	0	OPEN ROOM	0	LARGE EQPT	0
OTHER LOC	0	UNEVEN NO's	0	OTHER ORG	0	WHEELCHAIR	0
		OPEN GROUP	0			MUSIC	0
		OTHER FORM	0			OTHER EQPT	0
ACTIVITY:		INTENTION:		EXPERIENCE:		DESCRIPTION:	
WALK/RUN	0	COMMUNICATION	0	BODY AWARE	0		
CATCH/THROW	0	INTERACTION	0	MAT AWARE	0	GAME IDEA	0
SING/DANCE	0	RELAXATION	0	SOCIAL EXP	0	GAME RULES	0
EXPRESSION	0	COMPETITION	0	_____		VARIATION	0
EQPT ACTIVITY	0	PROJECT GAME	0	SUITABLE FOR		EQPT CONSTR	0
OTHER ACTIVITY	0	OTHER INTENT	0	WHEELCHAIR	0	REMARKS	0

Here are the criteria for the individual categories:

- **Location:**
  Gymnasium (wall-bars, multi-gym, marked-out pitch ...); field (sports field, grassed area ...); open ground (wood, meadow); water (indoor, outdoor, paddling pool ...).

- **Social Form:**
  Individual; with a partner; small groups (3-12 people); teams; uneven numbers; open groups.

- **Organisation:**
  Games in a circle; relay games; pitch (hard surfaced); open room.

- **Material/Equipment:**
  Balls (all sizes, colours ...); gymnasium equipment (hoops, little ropes, swinging clubs, ribbons); psychomotor equipment (trolley boards, pedal-vehicles, sheets ...); large equipment (trampoline, giant air bed, gymnastics equipment); wheelchairs; music.

- **Activity:**
  Walking/running (all forms of forward movement including hopping, jumping, swimming...); catching/throwing (catching and throwing, rushing and stopping); singing/dancing; expression (all forms of expressive activity); equipment activity (moving with equipment).

- **Intention:**
  Communication (games which lend themselves to getting to know each other, talking amongst each other); interaction (games which have co-operation as the main principle); relaxation; competition; project games.

- **Experience:**
  Awareness of the body; equipment awareness; social experience.

- **Suitable for Wheelchair:**
  This category includes the games which can be played in the wheelchair.

In the appendix all the games described in this book are compiled into a data bank, divided into categories according to the criteria above. This makes it possible to look up for example aquatic games, games suitable for the wheelchair or games for body-awareness. There are also many possibilities to combine the various games, so that a criterion can be combined with a different category e.g., ball games in water, or gymnasium games with psychomotor exercise equipment for awareness.

The data bank was assembled in the framework of the project "Movement, Games and Sports for Disabled Children and Youths", and was carried out with the co-operation of the Ministry of Culture North Rhine Westphalia at the University/Polytechnic of Paderborn. In the meanwhile the data bank has been expanded and improved and is available on CD-Rom in a multi-media version in the German language.

I. Integrated Family Sport

Part 1:   Movement, Games and Sports for the whole Family

The games and exercise forms described in this section are designed to show all the things that can be done jointly, and what can be organised for integrated family sport together with disabled and able bodied people. At the same time many of these games provide a stimulus for laying on leisure activities at home.

The games (and exercises) can form the beginning of the sports afternoon. In this way they serve the purpose of warming-up exercises, and provide preparation for the sporting stresses of the sports session, and the aim and purpose of particular themes and targets. They can also be used as an introduction to the planned activities.

Many of the games and exercise forms can be used to provide individual main themes such as "family games" or "ball games" in the main section of the sports session. Furthermore a large part of the games are suitable for ending a session of family sport.

1. Running and Chasing Games

Chain Catch
Rules of the Game:
The catcher begins catching. Each person he[1] catches, joins hands with him so that gradually a long chain is formed. Only the free hands of the two outside (end) players can be used to catch anyone.

Variation:
   • When the chain has reached a total of ten people it can split into two groups.

Catching and Freeing
Rules of the Game:
One, two or three catchers – depending on the size of the group – try to catch as many people as they can. The people caught have to form a bridge, a bank or stand there with legs straddled outwards. They can be 'freed' by people not yet caught by going under the bridge.

Variations:
   • Increase the number of catchers.
   • Type of bridge, bank, the way the legs are apart, bank designs ...
   • In the wheelchair: freeing by shaking hands or tapping the back of the wheelchair.
   • In water: freeing by diving through the straddled legs.

Magic Mouse
Rules of the Game:
A cat is the catcher. It tries to catch the mice. Mice who have been caught must stand still and raise one arm to show they are caught. Amongst the mice there is a magic mouse who can free the others by tipping them on the back secretly. The magic mouse is chosen beforehand without the cat being present. The game is over when the magic mouse has been caught.

Variations:
   • Two magic mice.
   • Two or more cats.
   • The magic mice have a particular characteristic e.g., red trousers.
   • Nicholas is the magic mouse, or all people with beards can free the mice.

Statues

Rules of the Game:
The catcher tries to catch all the others. Anyone who is tagged has to stand still in the position he was caught in like a statue. He is freed by a person not yet caught who takes him by the hand and turns him about in a circle.

Variations:
- Two, three or more catchers depending on the size of the group.
- Freeing can happen when two players, not yet caught, circle or hug the caught person.

On the Spot

Rules of the Game:
The catcher begins to catch. The person caught must hold the spot on his body where he was touched, and becomes the new catcher.

Variations:
- Two or more catchers.
- The number of catchers increases as those caught become catchers.

Chain Catch in Pairs

Rules of the Game:
The catcher catches a partner. They carry on as partners catching together. Those caught join into pairs and carry on catching until soon all are catching in pairs. This game is also possible by forming two teams, or forming pairs, without a great deal of organisational bother.

Black and White – or – Day and Night

Rules of the Game:
Two equal sized groups sit approximately 2 m away from and opposite each other on the middle line of the gymnasium floor. When an acoustic signal is given (a call – black or white) and/or a visible signal is given (white or black flag) the team called tries to catch the other team. Players can only be caught in an area up to a maximum of 3-5 m away from the gymnasium side-walls (marked by a line).

Variations:
- The way of starting the game can be changed: legs stretched out, lying on the back, lying on the stomach, shoulder stand, eyes closed ...

- The signal can be: a black or white disc which is thrown; calling out and pointing in a direction to move in as well; only an acoustic signal ...
- A story can be told in which the keyword 'black' or 'white' crops up.

Guardian of the Bridge

Rules of the Game:
The bridge guard is the catcher between two little huts which represent the bridge. Everyone else must cross over the bridge and change sides before the catcher can tag them.

Variations:
- Always only one bridge guard, the person caught last becomes the new bridge guard.
- The number of bridge guards increases because all those caught become bridge guards.
- Everyone runs, hops, goes on one leg or goes on all fours.
- Everyone can only cross the bridge in pairs.

Chain Catch in Threes

Rules of the Game:
The catcher starts. People caught hold onto the catcher until a group of more than three people is formed and then it breaks up. They carry on catching people in threes until all persons have been caught. In this way for example groups of threes can be chosen.

ABC-Catch

Rules of the Game:
All move round the hall in groups of threes. The three people in the group run or walk closely together. Each person in the group gets a name A, B or C. When the sports leader calls out A for Anthony, then A runs away and B and C join hands and try to catch A. After that all three run around closely together until for example C for Celia is called out and then A and B try to catch her.

Variations:
- A, B and C run, hop or skip around.
- Running backwards or sideways.
- Go around on all fours.
- The letters not called out e.g., B and C have to link arms before they catch A.

Who's Afraid of the Water Sprite?

(see Aquatic Games for description)

Reaction Game

Rules of the Game:

Everyone runs around in the hall. When the signal is given everyone has to react correctly.

Clap hands once — lay down on the stomach.

Clap hands twice — sit down.

Clap hands three times — lay down on the back.

Variations:

• Vary the way of moving: running, hopping, skipping, running forwards, sideways, backwards, galloping sideways and running on all fours ...

• Begin with a signal and then change over after the third signal.

• Use other signals such as a whistle; standing on one leg, stamping the foot; lie down, frog noises or snapping one's fingers; go on all fours.

• For wheelchairs: move into a corner of the room, balancing on two wheels, come together in the middle, drive onto a mat and other exercises.

Fire, Water and Air

Rules of the Game:

Everyone runs, hops or jumps around the hall. When one of the words 'fire', 'water' or 'air' is called out the following actions must be carried out immediately. 'fire' = run into the corner, 'water' = get off the ground quickly e.g., climb up the wall-bars or onto benches etc., 'air' = lie down flat.

Variations:

• Change the way of going around.

• As a fourth signal: "Save yourselves!" – for this call, you try to jump onto someone else's back – piggyback.

• For wheelchairs: move into a corner of the room, balancing on two wheels, come together in the middle, drive onto a mat.

Catching the Tail

Rules of the Game:

All participants have a team ribbon tucked into the back of the trousers so that at least half of the ribbon is hanging out. Everyone then runs about trying to catch as many tails as they can.

Variations:
- Who got the most tails? All players stay in the game.
- Who kept his tail for the longest?
- Whoever loses his tail, can replace it with one caught. When you do not have a tail any longer, you drop out.

Catching Elephants
Rules of the Game:
The catcher holds his nose with his left hand. He now pushes his right hand through the 'eyelet' formed and creates an elephant's trunk. In this position the elephant catches the others. Everyone caught becomes the elephant.

Variations:
- One catcher at a time.
- The number of catchers (elephants) increases as the person caught joins the elephant as a further catcher.
- Everyone runs backwards, sideways ...

Jets and Gliders
Rules of the Game:
At the cry of 'jets' all the children run around the hall screeching and whistling like a jet aircraft with their arms spread out behind them. In contrast they go around on the call of 'glider' slowly and quietly with their arms stretched out sideways.

'Help me!'
Rules of the Game:
The catcher tries to catch the others. If someone is in danger of being caught he can call out 'Help me!' Someone else can then hold his hand. These two can then not be caught. The catcher has to find another 'victim'. In spite of this if someone is caught he becomes the new catcher.

Variations:
- Two or more catchers.
- One catcher starts. Anyone caught becomes an additional catcher so that the number of catchers always increases.
- The way of moving around is varied: running, hopping, running backwards, using a wheelchair.

Variations:
- The number of hunters can be increased.
- The hunters are not allowed to run with the ball.
- The hunters are allowed only to throw from particular positions e.g., with a foot on a line on the hall floor, with one hand holding the head, throwing backwards through the legs ...

Scotland Yard

Rules of the Game:
Several detectives try to catch Mr X. All the detectives are blind, with their eyes closed and positioned, separated out throughout the hall. Mr X takes two paces, after which all the detectives, when told to go by the game leader, also can take two paces towards the direction where they think Mr X is. If Mr X is in danger he can call on three joker cards i.e., he can take four paces instead of two. When the detectives touch Mr X then he is caught.

Variation:
- Mr X has an additional joker card i.e., he can go underground: e.g., in the swimming pool he can swim underwater as far as he likes.

2.   Ball Games

2.1   Simple Ball Games for Everyone

Keep the Crate Full

Rules of the Game:
One or two baskets in the middle are full of balls. Two parents or exercise leaders try to throw the balls out of the basket as quickly as possible. All the other members of the sports group collect up the balls and throw them back into the basket again. If they get all the balls in the basket then they have won. If the baskets are emptied then the "throwers" have won.

Variation:
- Four baskets of balls in the four corners of the hall, each with different coloured balls: red, white, green and blue. Each colour must be thrown back into the correct basket.

Keep the Side Clear _____

Rules of the Game:
The hall is divided into two halves using benches or a rope. A team occupies each half and as far as possible each player has at least one ball. On a mutual signal each team tries to keep its playing area free of balls by throwing all reachable balls into the other half. At a signal given by the referee no more balls may be thrown. The team wins who has the least number of balls in its area.

Variations:
• The balls are rolled.
• The balls are rolled through the legs.
• The balls can only be thrown backwards.

Ball under the Rope _____

Rules of the Game:
A rope (placed 2 ft high) divides the volleyball pitch into two playing halves. Each team has the task to throw the ball under the rope so that it rolls over the other teams rear baseline thus scoring a goal.

Variations:
• Different balls: volleyball, handball, medicine ball, rugby ball etc.
• Distance between the baseline and the side lines can be varied.
• Breadth of the goal can be varied e.g., using little cones.

Rolling the Ball _____

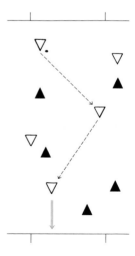

Rules of the Game:
Two teams play with a basketball or medicine ball i.e., they may only roll the ball with the hand and are not allowed to throw it. The goals are formed by two benches laid on their side against which the ball must be rolled.

Diagram 2: Rolling the ball

Variations:
- Size of the playing area.
- Size of the goal (e.g., two benches).
- Team size.
- Different types of ball.

Throwing through the Hoop

Rules of the Game:
Each couple of one half of the group has a hoop and they run around the hall with it. Each of the other players has a ball which he tries to throw through as many hoops as possible. After 3-5 minutes the roles are changed.

Variations:
- Use bags of rice.
- Holding the hoops up above the head.

Rolling Hoops down the Lane

Rules of the Game:
One team tries to roll their hoops down a lane, formed for example by benches. The other team stands down both sides of the lane and tries to knock down the hoops as they roll past. Each hoop to reach its goal gets a point and can be rolled down the lane again. When all hoops have been knocked out, roles can be changed.

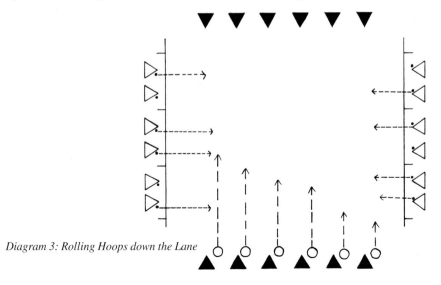

Diagram 3: Rolling Hoops down the Lane

Variations:
- Throwers use handballs, softballs or bags of rice.
- Hits are counted according to a predetermined number of hoops that can be rolled.

Tired, Worn out, Dead

Rules of the Game:
The group forms circles of 6-12 persons. Each circle has a ball thrown into it. The first time a person does not catch it, he is called 'tired' i.e., he kneels down. The second time he does not catch it he is 'worn out' i.e., he sits down. The third time he does not catch it he is 'dead' i.e., he lies down and drops out.

Variations:
- In water: tired = ducking down up to the shoulders in water; worn out = up to the chin in water; dead = under the water and out.
- One-handed catching and throwing.
- Call out the name before throwing.
- Clapping the hands together before catching the ball.

2.2   Hunter Ball Games

Simple Hunter Ball

Rules of the Game:
The hunter, identifiable by a coloured ribbon (when in the water by his bathing cap), tries to hit the hares with a softball. Every hare hit turns into a hunter and gets a ribbon to wear. When there are more than three hunters they may not run with the ball any more and have the ball thrown to them.

Variations:
- Several softballs.
- Hares run around on all fours.
- The hunters must throw with two hands.
- The hunters throw with the opposite hand to their usual (right-handed throw with the left hand).

Reverse Hunter Ball

Rules of the Game:
All players start off as hunters (all wearing a ribbon). There is only one hare left. Every hunter who hits a hare turns into a hare until all are hares and only one hunter is left.

Hunter Ball vs. Animal Rights Supporters

Rules of the Game:
A hunter (wearing a ribbon) tries to hit the hares. But there are 3-5 animal rights supporters, who protect the hares and may deflect the balls.

Variations:
* More hunters.
* The number of hunters increases as the hares hit turn into hunters.

Hunters and Crabs

Rules of the Game:
Two hunters try to hit the hares with a softball. Every hare hit turns into a crab i.e., he has to run on all fours backwards and tries to touch the hares who also turn into crabs.

Never-ending Hunter Ball

Rules of the Game:
Only the person in possession of the ball is the hunter. He is allowed to run three paces with the ball. Hares who are hit have to sit on the floor and are 'dead' until they, by chance, get hold of the ball. They are then the hunter because whoever has the ball is the hunter. This game can go on for ever because everyone can become the hunter or the hare and the hares hit can rejoin the game as the hunter. Hunters can also deliberately steer the ball towards the hares in order to allow them to be freed.

The Hare Drive

Rules of the Game:
One half of the group are the hunters and spread themselves evenly around the hall. The other half of the group are the hares. They stand with a softball at one end of the hall. A hare throws the ball into the field. At the same time all the hares run to the other end. As they do the hunters try to hit as many hares as possible. The hits are counted up. All the hares stay in the game. After 4-6 goes the roles are switched over. The hares are now the hunters and the hunters become the hares. The winners are the group who, when hunters, score the most hits.

Variations:
* Two, three or more softballs.
* The hares have to hop to the other side; run on all fours.
* Hares who are hit drop out. How many attempts does it take to have no more hares?

2.3   Group Ball Games

Simple Group Ball Game

Rules of the Game:
Two teams in two different halves of the hall try to throw the ball to each other amongst themselves as often as possible without someone preventing them from doing so. Which team manages to pass the ball more times without the ball dropping on the ground is the winner.

Variations:
- The teams stand in a circle.
- The teams run around amongst themselves in their own half.
- One or two people from the other group can try to prevent or deflect the ball being passed.

The Ten Pass Game

Rules of the Game:
Two even teams, identifiable by wearing ribbons, play against each other by trying to keep the ball passing amongst themselves in the same team. If they succeed in passing the ball ten times without the opposition touching the ball they get a point. If the opposing team captures the ball beforehand, then they try to pass the ball ten times. After ten successful passes in the same team then the ball is handed over to the opposition for them to try to make a point.

Variations:
- After five or six passes a point is awarded.
- No running with the ball; maximum of two paces (basketball) or three paces (handball).
- Dribbling is allowed.
- The ball cannot be passed back to the thrower.

The Ten Pass Game with an Additional Point

Rules of the Game:
The same rules as the ten-pass game above, but after the ten passes an additional point can be awarded by hitting a target. Targets can be e.g., hoops lying on the side of the playing area (e.g., four red hoops and four blue hoops).

Variations:
- Team members may only target the colour of their team ribbon.
- The basketball target can be used – backboard one point; a basket two points.
- Skittles standing on benches at the end of the hall have to be knocked off.
- In water: swimming floats standing on the pool-side have to be knocked down (two floats leaning against each other); water-polo goals or water basketball goals can be used as targets for the additional point.

2.4   Fire Ball

Fire Ball

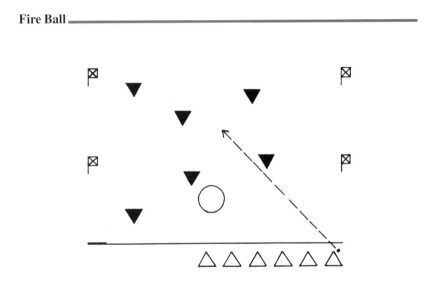

Diagram 4: Fire Ball

Rules of the Game:
One team is the throwing side and stands behind a baseline. One of the players in this team tries to throw the ball so that the other team has difficulty in catching it and throwing it quickly into the home base. While they are trying to do this the thrower runs around the field. He can stop at each flag-post. If he is able to run round the whole field and get back to the baseline then he is awarded three points. If he can do it in stages he gets one point. If the ball hits the home base before the runner reaches a flag-post, he is 'burnt' and is awarded no points. When each team member has thrown once or twice then the points are added up and the roles switch over i.e., the fielders switch over to be throwers and vice versa.

Variations:
- The fielders must pass the ball three times.
- The runners have to hop round or go on pedal-vehicles, in which case the distance between the flag-posts will have to be reduced.
- The fielders have to hit the basketball backboard.
- The basketball basket is the home base.
- The runners have to go round in a wheelchair.

2.5 'Völker-Ball'

'Völker-Ball'[2] – Basic Game

Rules of the Game:
Two teams stand in their playing areas opposite each other. One player (the king) on each side stands behind the opposing team. One team now tries, in co-operation with their own 'king', to hit as many members of the other team as possible. Those hit directly must join their 'king' on the baseline. Balls that are caught or touch the ground do not count. When all the players have been hit the 'king' comes onto the playing area. He has 'three lives' and must be hit three times. The winner is the team who gets all the others out first.

Variations:
- Use two hands to throw.
- The right arm is taboo: only the opposite hand to normal can be used to throw (right-handed people to use the left hand).
- Play the game with more than one softball.

Reverse 'Völker-Ball'

Rules of the Game:
All the players stand behind the baseline with each team having one player in the playing area. Each player who scores a hit can come into the playing area. The player hit also stays in the playing area. Which team is the first complete in the playing area?

'Völker-Ball' – Freeing

Rules of the Game:
Play 'Völker-Ball' – basic game, but this time any player that is hit can 'free' himself. If he hits an opponent he can rejoin the playing area.

Three-Sided 'Völker-Ball'

Rules of the Game:
Throwing the ball to strike the opposing team can also be carried out from the sideline.
In this way the opposing team is threatened from three sides of the playing area.

Obstacle Course – 'Völker-Ball'

Rules of the Game:
Obstacles such as boxes, vaulting horses are placed in the playing area and players can
hide behind them. Other rules as per of the basic game of 'Völker-Ball' – Freeing.

'Völker-Ball' with Skittles

Rules of the Game:
Each player places a skittle (or cone) in the playing area that he has to defend. If the
skittle is hit or is knocked over because the player is clumsy then he is out. Other rules
as per the basic game or of 'Völker-Ball' – Variations.

'Völker-Ball' – Three Playing Areas

Rules of the Game:
This is played with three teams in three playing areas. The two outside teams now try
to hit the middle team.

Variations:
- Which team, playing in the middle, avoids the most hits in a time of five minutes?
  (No-one drops out! – change sides after five minutes.)
- Which team, playing in the middle, holds out the longest? Players hit drop out. The
  time is read from a stopwatch when the last player in the middle team is hit. After
  this – change sides.

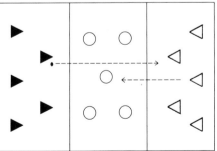

Diagram 5: 'Völker-Ball'– three playing areas

2.6   Ball over the Rope

Ball over the Rope – Basic Game ━━━━━━━━━━━━━━━━━━━━━━━━━━━━━━━

Rules of the Game:
The ball is played by two teams so that it goes over a rope, strung up high, with the idea that it falls and hits the ground. This scores one point. The pitch is marked out like the volleyball pitch or smaller.

Variations:
- Team sizes: 3 versus 3; up to 6 versus 6 or more.
- Different balls: balloons, softballs, medicine balls, rugby balls, indiaca (a pear-shaped ball with three coloured feathers – played like volleyball), frisbees, volleyballs.
- Rules:
  - Players running and throwing the ball anyhow.
  - Players not allowed to run with the ball.
  - Only three contacts allowed before the ball must be played over the rope.
  - Only a limited time allowed for holding the ball.
  - Match the size of the pitch to the number of players.
  - Size of the pitch as per volleyball.
  - Introduce volleyball rules in gradual stages.

3.   Games with Music, Singing and Joining Hands

Many of the following games illustrated are particularly suitable to get a sports session moving in a lively manner with lots of rhythm and music. The exercises can be organised so that new families are afforded an easy introduction to the activities and that things are made easy for conversation to flourish. In this way new contacts can be built up.

One or two of the singing games will already be familiar to disabled children from school. Thus they can bring their experience into play in the session.

It is also possible to organise the whole of the sports session by using games with music, singing and games. A good opportunity for this is when a new group meets for the first time or when an existing family group invites another group as guests. The end of a sports session gives another opportunity for these games to be used to good effect.

3.1   Games to Music

The Welcome Game ━━━━━━━━━━━━━━━━━━━━━━━━━━━━━━━━━━

Rules of the Game:

Everyone moves around the gymnasium to the rhythm of the music. The way one moves can be varied: running, skipping, hopping, jumping, running backwards, galloping sideways, going on all fours and other ways of moving which could match the corresponding music. When the music stops everyone must carry out an exercise to express a welcome or other greeting.

Variations:

- Shake hands with as many as possible.
- Introduce as many people to each other as possible.
- Greet as many other people as possible in a different way: a slap on the shoulder, shake hands or feet, a hug, rub noses like the Eskimos ...
- Start a conversation with someone.
- Do a short interview of as many people as possible.
- Choice of music: lively and rhythmical music that matches running or hopping.

The Molecular Game ━━━━━━━━━━━━━━━━━━━━━━━━━━━━━━━━━

Rules of the Game:

In this game everyone moves round the whole of the gymnasium to the rhythm of the music. When the music stops the exercise leader calls out, or indicates visibly, that the groups have to form into certain sizes e.g., fours, five's ... eight's etc. The groups now have to carry out certain tasks about different topics.

- Communication; getting to know one another:
  - Ask each other their name.
  - Get into conversation.
  - Interview the others about certain themes: sports interests, hobbies.
  - Carry out a discussion about certain themes such as leisure.
- Physical exercises:
  - Move about as a group.
  - Which group can form up to take up the smallest space?
  - Which group can form up to take up the most space?
  - Which group can build the best and most creative tower (not the highest)?
  - The group sits down with their backs to each other and tries to push themselves up into a standing position without using their hands.

- The group makes up something using the group members, which the others have to guess.e.g., monument, a submarine, an aeroplane, a flower in bloom ...
- Carry out other creative exercises such as e.g., a group of five have to form up so that only three of all their legs are touching the ground – likewise in a group of seven only four legs and three hands can touch the ground etc.

After each exercise the group disperses and each person moves about to the music in the room, using different methods of movement: forwards, backwards, sideways, running, skipping, jumping, hopping, sideways gallop, on one leg, on all fours, run as fast as possible or as slowly as possible e.g., slow motion.

Picture 5: Moving about in the 'Molecular Game' – going around as a group.

Dancing with Balloons

Rules of the Game:

At the beginning of the session everyone is given a balloon and has to blow it up. He now writes his name and draws a unique symbol (e.g., a tree or a flower etc.,) on it with a felt tip pen. Now everyone moves around in the hall to the music with their balloon. The way of moving about can be:

Variations:
- Hold the balloon with only one hand; knocking it forward.
- Hold the balloon up in the air using different parts of the body.
- Move the balloon around together with a partner.
- Hold the balloon between your own and a partner's body and go around like that.
- Your partner stands 5 m away from you – each hits his balloon high up into the air and each has to run after the partner's balloon and catch it before it hits the ground.
- Get to know as many other partners as possible (keeping to name and symbol categories).
- Choice of music: slow and solemn music alternating with somewhat faster tempo.

Shake Hands

Rules of the Game:
In this 'welcoming' game, each person decides how many times he will shake the other person's hand (1-5 times). The aim is now to find out how many other people have decided on the same number of times to shake hands. Like numbers form into a group.

Variation:
- Change the way of greeting: tap someone on the shoulder, hug each other, bow to each other (Asian greeting), Eskimo greeting, wink at each other ...

Statues
(Rules of the Game: see "Running and Chasing Games")

Frozen Rice Bags

Rules of the Game:
All move round the hall balancing a bag of rice on the head. If the rice bag falls down you have to stand still – freeze – until someone else picks it up and places it on your head again.

Variations:
- Place the rice bag on different parts of the body: left shoulder, elbow, back of the right hand, left knee ...
- Vary the way of moving: walk, run, skip, run backwards, run down a marked line in the hall.
- Choice of music: slow and solemn music alternating with somewhat faster tempo.

Copy-cat

Rules of the Game:

Everyone finds a partner. The partner moves around the hall adopting different gaits as he goes. The other person follows him round like a shadow and copies his movements. After two or three minutes swap over the roles.

• Choice of music: lively rhythmical music to which one can easily run and skip.

Mirror

Rules of the Game:

You and your partner stand apart at a distance of 1-2 m from each other. The one partner now does a mirror reflection of all the other person's movements.

• Choice of music: first of all slow, swinging music, followed by more lively music.

Dancing Opposites

Rules of the Game:

Two of you (partners) stand in front of each other – like in front of a mirror. The other person must do exactly the opposite action to his partner. Start with simple actions and then move on to more difficult ones e.g., crossing the arms; crossing the legs; lying on the stomach; lying on the back; twisting the head round etc.

Dancing down the Line

Rules of the Game:

All the players move round the hall to music by going along the lines marked out. Meetings are only possible where lines cross – here one can evade other players.

Variations:

• All the marked out lines in the hall can be used.
• Only certain lines can be used: only the thick lines or only red lines or black lines.
• When you meet someone, you do not have to go back to a crossing – you can try to get past by balancing around each other, climb over each other or find another way to get past without leaving the line.

Playing Dollies

Rules of the Game:

Partners stand together. One of them acts being a clockwork-dolly, who when wound up dances and skips around without stopping until the partner finds the switch and turns the dolly off. The person starting has to think up beforehand which part of his body represents the switch e.g., right ear, belly-button or ... Then change over.

Variation:
   • Choice of music: rhythmical to 'choppy' music.

Popcorn

Rules of the Game:
The leader first of all tells a story: "Just imagine you are a grain of maize and you are sitting in the frying-pan all close together. Now the frying-pan is getting hotter. What does the maize do now it is getting hotter? Correct – it jumps – goes "pop" and has turned into popcorn. When it gets hot, we also jump up and skip around. But popcorn is sweet and sticky. Therefore we stick to whoever we are close to or bump into. In this way more and more persons gradually come together until we are all formed into skipping mass of sweet popcorn."

   • Choice of music: "Popcorn" or other similar music.

Picture 6: A great "big sweet mass of popcorn"

3.2 Games in a Circle/Joining Hands and Singing Games

At this juncture I want to introduce a few examples of English tunes and words used for circle and joining hands games. Naturally the reader will want to adapt his/her own country's popular children's nursery rhymes or songs to suit local wishes. Undoubtedly the players themselves will want to make their own suggestions and they should be allowed to do so to further co-operation and initiative.

"Up I Stretch"

Rules of the Game:
All stand in a circle singing "Up I Stretch" and do the actions indicated by the words. Everyone joins in the actions. One child in the centre of the circle skips past everybody. Afterwards the skipping child swaps with another child.

> Up I stretch on tippy toe,
> Down to touch my heels I go,
> Up again my arms I send,
> down again my knees I bend.

Variation:
• The first child joins in with the second child.

Stepping over Stepping Stones

Rules of the Game:
Children hop across 'stepping stones', improvised by rice bags or chalk marks.

> Stepping over stepping stones, One, two, three
> Stepping over stepping stones,
> come with me,
> The river's very fast,
> and the river's very wide,
> and we'll step across on stepping stones
> and reach the other side.

"Sometimes I'm Very Small"

Rules of the Game:
While the others sing one child covers his eyes and has to guess whether they are standing tall or crouching.

> Sometimes I'm very small
> sometimes I'm very tall
> Shut your eyes and turn around
> and guess which I am now.

- Run, carrying the ball stuck between the legs.
- And other ways of carrying the ball.

• **Moving the Ball:**
- Roll the ball with the hand.
- Roll the ball using the left foot.
- Dribbling with the ball.
- Carrying two or more balls.
- Roll one ball, carry the other one.
- Dribbling with one ball while carrying or rolling the second.
- Dribbling with the hand on the ball, the other ball with the foot.
- Moving several balls between two persons.
- Carrying three or more balls.
- Carrying the ball in different ways e.g., one ball in the left hand, one ball under the right arm, one ball between the legs.
- Carrying three balls, but only two balls can be touched (the third ball is held squashed between the other two).
- Other ways of carrying the ball.

• **Slalom relay races:**
- Carrying the ball as above but through a slalom made of cones or poles.
• **Obstacle relay races:**
- Relay races with various types of obstacle.
• **Relay races moving objects:**
- For example – rice bags, balloons ....

Scooter

Rules of the Game:
All the players form into groups of fours and these stand behind each other holding onto the front person's shoulders (or around the hips). The leading person leads the others who have their eyes closed. They steer around the room in different directions without hitting another group.

Variations:
• The second person in the group steers from his position.
• The third person in the group steers from his position.
• The last person in the group steers from his position.
• All use wheelchairs and hang onto each other.

The Gordian Knot/ Untying the Knot ━━━━━━━━━━━━━━━━━━━━━━

Rules of the Game:
One group forms a circle and joins hands. The group now 'makes a knot' by one part of the group creeping under the arms of another part, and another part of the same group stepping over the arms of yet another part – when the 'Gordian Knot' has been 'tied' the group starts to untie itself.

Variations:
- A member of the group, who is looking away or is sent out of the room while the group ties itself up, has to 'untie' the group.
- All players stand close together and hold their arms up in the air. Each person grasps hold of the two free hands. The 'Gordian Knot' that is formed is very difficult to 'untie'.

Further Games to Firm up the Body ━━━━━━━━━━━━━━━━━━━━━━

- Leap-frog
- Rolling the Hoop
- Games Using the Skipping Rope
- On the Spot

• Actions Involving the Whole Body and Climbing Obstacles ━━━━━━

Rules of the Game:
Basic abilities such as balancing, jumping, swinging, climbing etc., can be exercised best by using a varied programme of obstacle courses; (see chapter B.II.1). The aims, however, can also be achieved by exercises such as the Catching and Chasing Games, Copy-cat etc., (see chapter B.I.1).

• Improving Hand-eye Co-ordination ━━━━━━━━━━━━━━━━━━━━━━

The improvement of hand-eye co-ordination can best be achieved by using games that involve targeting with the hands. As described below, a simple game that uses the hand or foot to target with, is the 'Skittle Game' and is carried out in uncomplicated conditions and gives the unskilled child the best chance of some success at the same time.

Rules of the Game:
Skittles
Form a lane by using upturned benches. Various skittles or traffic cones are placed inside the area. The child now tries to knock over as many 'skittles' as possible using a ball. Because of the ricochet effect off the benches the chances of success are increased.

Variations:
- Use different balls: softball, handball, football, rugby ball, medicine ball.
- Angle the benches differently.
- For the severely disabled the ball can be rolled down a ramp.
- Kick the ball.

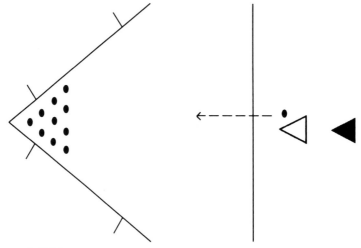

Diagram 6: Skittles

The Coconut Shy

Rules of the Game:
Set up two benches with 8-10 little cones standing on each. The teams now try and knock off as many cones as possible from a laid down distance.

Variation:
- Increase the distance between the two benches.
- Use different types of ball: soft ball, handball, football, rugby ball, medicine ball.
- Play one person versus another.
- Team game: two teams play against one another – team size (3-8 persons).
- Balls to be kicked at the cones .

- **Further games:**
  - Keep the Crate Full
  - Keep the Side Clear

- Hunter Ball Games
- 'Völker-Ball'
- Group Ball Games
- Rolling the Ball

• Acting Games

This theme can teach children to learn how to express body feelings using gestures and mime. This ranges from little imitation games and playing roles to complex acting out scenarios.

Let's Move like the Animals
Idea:
All the children move around the area like animals which the leader calls out (and possibly acts him/herself): frog, stork, bear, tiger, duck etc.

Animal Movements to Music
Idea:
The music indicates, either from the melody or the rhythm, which animal should be used to copy.

Activities from Daily Life
Idea:
Examples: singing and acting - "Jack and Jill went up the hill"
                            - "What shall we do with the drunken sailor?"

Acting out Feelings
Idea:
Act like animals experiencing various feelings: fear, tummy-ache, joy ...

Feather-weights
Idea:
Two children play together – one is a feather who is blown or tapped around by the other child.

Variation:
• One of the children shakes the cushion (bed sheet) and lots of "feathers" (i.e., children) drop out e.g., the children tumble out from under the sheet. The harder the sheet is shaken the more the feathers (children) fly about.

Games with Other Psychomotor Exercise Equipment

Rules of the Game:

Many other so-called "psychomotor exercise equipment" are suitable for use in family sport. They are only briefly mentioned here, as to include all the forms of each of the games and exercises with them, would reach well over the bounds of this book:

- Therapeutic gyro equipment
- Spastic balls
- Balancing ropes
- Crawling tunnels
- Tube-slides
- Sheets (see next section: Parachute)

The Parachute

There is hardly any other piece of equipment that is more suitable to stimulate heterogeneous groups to participate in joint activities than the parachute. The parachute allows little children, larger children, youths and grown-ups to all play together – disabled and able bodied as well as active professional and amateur leisure sportsmen and women can exercise and gain experience with this equipment.

Picture 8: "All the yellow triangles change places with all the numbers 3 and 5"

If there is a parachute available that is multicoloured – even one that has been painted by the group – then there is a lot more than just joint games that can be learned; basic terms such as colours, forms and numbers can be taught and learned.

In a leisure session for families a normal white parachute, that had been written-off, was coloured by the group using silk-screen coloured ink. The 24 segments now have different colours, forms and shapes drawn on them. The forms of the circle, square and triangle have been painted in the four basic colours red, yellow, green and blue as well as the figures 1-6, also in the four colours. Exercises can be carried out in conjunction with the different colours, forms and numbers.

From all the possibilities for games with the parachute the following are particularly suitable for a family sports group. Most of these games can also be done with a sheet.

Making Waves

Rules of the Game:
All the members of the family sports group position themselves around the parachute, grasping it in their hands. By raising the hands slowly up and down, waves are created in the parachute surface.

Variations:
- Standing still: make smaller or bigger waves.
- Walking: everyone holds onto the parachute with the right hand. The group now begins to circle around making waves as they go.
- Change direction.
- The group not only goes around in circles but chooses other directions to go about.
- Change the way of moving: walking, running, skipping, side-gallop.

The Giant Mushroom

Rules of the Game:
All crouch down and swing the parachute up so that it rises, and at the same time they also rise up themselves until they are standing. The next time they try to get it to rise higher.

Variations:
- Making the mushroom while standing still.
- Making the mushroom while moving: each person grasps the parachute in the right hand. The group begins to circle around and makes the parachute into a mushroom as they go.

- Change direction.
- The group does not only go around in circles but chooses other directions to go about.
- Change the way of moving: walking, running, skipping, side-gallop.

Changing Sides

Rules of the Game:
When the parachute is up in the air, one section of the group runs under the parachute to change sides. Examples:

Variations:
- Everyone with the colour red in front of them.
- Everyone with a yellow circle in front of them.
- All the triangles.
- Everyone with the numbers 1,2 or 3 ...
- Everyone wearing white gym shoes.
- Everyone wearing blue track-suit bottoms.
- All the children or – all the grown-ups ...

The Parachute and the Balloon

Rules of the Game:
Several balloons are laid down on the parachute. All begin to move the parachute and watch the different movements they make when creating waves, or doing the mushroom and other games.

Variations:
- Try to keep the balloons still on the parachute as long as possible.
- Try to knock the balloons off the parachute as quickly as possible.

The Parachute and Balls

Rules of the Game:
First of all everyone tries to get a ball lying on the parachute to roll in different directions.

Variations:
- Try to get the ball to run round the edge of the parachute in a circle.
- This game is more interesting using two or more balls. Aim of the game is to keep the ball on the parachute.

- Try to knock the balls off the opposite side of the parachute by moving it in different directions.
- Try to throw balls off the other colours than one's own, and similarly avoid having 'goals' scored against you.

The Parachute and Rice-Bags

Rules of the Game:
Various differently coloured rice-bags are divided around the surface of the parachute. By making the wave movements the rice-bags are made to hop up and down which is quite amusing to watch.

Variations:
- Try to keep as many rice bags as possible on the parachute.
- Try to knock all the rice bags off the parachute as quickly as possible.
- Which colour rice bag stays on the parachute the longest?

Games under the Parachute

Rules of the Game:
A part of the group (e.g., all the children or all the ladies ...) lies down under the parachute. The others now create waves and a rush of air (wind). Those lying under the parachute close their eyes and try to feel the wind. Now the others create the "giant mushroom". The people under the parachute open their eyes and try to match the movement of the parachute i.e., when the parachute has risen up, everyone is stretching up as high as possible – when the parachute is dropping down they all quickly lie down again.

Visit to the Cathedral (or Go into the Igloo)

Rules of the Game:
All the participants swing the parachute up as high as possible (see "Giant Mushroom"). Everyone takes one step forward into the middle. On the third time that the parachute is swung up they can take another step into the middle and then pull the edge of the parachute down and sit on it inside. Now everyone is sitting inside the dome – like in a cathedral or an igloo.

Picture 9:The children under the parachute adapt to its movements.

Crocodile on the Nile

Rules of the Game:

A story is told for this game: "Let us imagine that we are in Africa. We have been going along for a long time and we have got really hot. We now arrive at a lovely lake (make waves with the parachute). Of course we sit down on the lakeside and paddle our feet in the water (everyone sits down and slip their legs under the parachute). Oh how lovely this is! Now, in the African waters there are dangerous animals like crocodiles. (Meanwhile, one of the players has crept under the parachute as the "crocodile" and he can pull the 'unsuspecting tourists' into the water. Each tourist that is eaten up turns into a crocodile.) Each tourist caught by a crocodile disappears into the water screaming until everyone has disappeared under the parachute.

Launching the Parachute

Rules of the Game:

After the group has made three sweep-ups with the parachute for the "Giant Mushroom", they let go of it and see how high they can launch it.

Variations:
- Before the parachute touches the ground again, everyone has to adopt particular positions; sit down, form a bridge, shoulder stand, three people sit down together back to back ...
- By the time the parachute has touched the ground, everyone has run away as far as they can.

Running with the Parachute

Rules of the Game:
This game is very suitable to play in the open-air, on the sports pitch and also in a large gymnasium:

Using the Parachute as a Roof: Three exercise supervisors or parents run with the parachute billowing up behind them. Everyone tries to run behind them sheltering under the parachute and seeing how long they can stay under it.

Variation: • Change direction frequently.

Using the Parachute as a Catching Net: Three grown-ups run with the parachute flying up behind them. Everyone runs away. Anybody who gets under the parachute is caught and joins in pulling the parachute as a catcher.

   Catching the Parachute: The grown-ups run with the parachute. The children try to catch the parachute.

Parachute Wrapping

Rules of the Game:
Several children wrap themselves up in the parachute.

Touching and Guessing

Rules of the Game:
Two players from the family sports group leave the gym for a short time or shut their eyes. One or two others hide inside the parachute and the catchers have to guess by touching.

Variations:
- The two catchers have to guess who is under the parachute.
- The two catchers have to feel what position the two under the parachute have adopted and copy it.

4.3   Games to Gain Social Experience

The aim of games to gain social experience is to develop the individual's ability to be social and provide a stimulus for this e.g., the person, the child or the disabled must be able to come to terms with the environment he lives in, be able to make contact with others, hold a conversation and to be able to do something jointly.

This is often much easier to accomplish during sports and games than with other activities. Thus games to do with communication and interactivity are important and valuable in this respect.

Opportunities to make contact and carry on conversations can be used to benefit both before or after family sports sessions as well as during them. This is especially so when the preparedness to do this has been preceded by carrying out these communicative activities during the exercises, and thus creating an open atmosphere and mutual understanding. Contacts can be broadened by carrying on with these activities over and above the 'normal family sport sessions' e.g., during family leisure outings, hikes and festivals etc.

Because there is almost an inexhaustible number of games which can be applied to this theme, in this section only the main points will be examined by illustrating a few examples. For further information see Games - Data Bank.

Leading the Blind

Rules of the Game:
This game requires absolute trust in the partner. One partner leads the other, who is blindfolded, around the gymnasium and over obstacles, using a variety of aids (using both hands and guiding – giving verbal explanations how and where to go).

Variations:
- Lead the 'blind' partner using only one hand or only with the tips of the fingers.
- Lead the partner using only verbal commands.
- Lead the partner by using prearranged signals e.g., tapping on the right shoulder = a 90° turn to the right, tapping on both shoulders = Stop!
- Lead the 'blind' partner by using a humming sound.
- Both partners close their eyes, and using a prearranged sound find each other.
- Hide and seek: everyone closes their eyes and tries to find the exercise supervisor who has hidden himself somewhere in the gymnasium. Anyone finding him sits down next to him.

Circle of Confidence

Rules of the Game:
4-6 players stand round together in a circle. One player stands in the middle and lets himself fall against the outside players. They catch him and push him back upright.

Variation:
• The player in the middle closes his eyes.

Dead Man

Rules of the Game:
One of the players lies down stiffly stretched out on the ground. Six players line up alongside the player and pick him up and carry him around the hall, holding him at differing heights. If the person being carried closes his eyes the feeling is more intense.

Variations:
• Carry him, holding him at different heights.
• Move at different speeds around the hall while carrying him.

Dance of the Magnets

Rules of the Game:
All the players dance on the lines in the hall to the rhythm of the music. The players are magnets with either a positive or a negative charge. When they get near another player they either are attracted to each other or are pushed away from each other.

Some of the other Games with Music:
• The Welcome Game
• The Molecular Game
• Dancing with Balloons
• Copy-cat
• Mirror
• Playing Dollies
• Popcorn

Games with the Main Aim of Communication and Interactivity from the Section
"Catching and Chasing Games" ▬▬▬▬▬▬▬▬▬▬▬▬▬▬▬▬▬▬
- "Help me!"
- Ball Possession – Taboo
- Catching and Freeing
- Magic Mouse
- Statues
- Frozen Rice Bags

Ball Games ▬▬▬▬▬▬▬▬▬▬▬▬▬▬▬▬▬▬▬▬▬▬▬▬▬▬▬▬
- Group Ball Game
- Never-ending Hunter Ball
- Other Little Ball Games

5. Gymnastics and Dancing

On the one hand, gymnastics and dancing are suitable forms of exercise for the introductory phases of family sports group sessions. On the other hand, dancing together is useful for bringing a sporting activity session to a close. This is why dancing, which can be jointly carried out – by the smallest child to the oldest participant – is often used to close our family sports sessions.

Dancing and gymnastics can also form the main part of a sports session, especially as an activity for target groups or parts of these; often the ladies target group requests a particular dance or chooses a special gymnastic activity such as aerobics or exercises for the spinal cord. The ladies in our family sports group have used these opportunities, during normal sports sessions, to rehearse dances that they perform at carnivals or other events.

5.1 Gymnastics

Gymnastics can be brought in for the whole group as little interludes, between the games, in the introductory part of the sports session. Particularly suitable are gymnastics with equipment such as hoops, ropes or balls – above all this is beneficial when the equipment will be used also in games, either before or afterwards. Gymnastic exercises can also be interjected into the content of individual games – e.g., gymnastics which can be introduced into the "Molecular game" could be: 'Find an exercise form to strengthen the stomach muscles or to loosen the joints in the shoulders, and demonstrate these to everyone else!'

Games and Gymnastics with Hoops

Simple games and gymnastics with hoops can be put together to music so that an enjoyable sequence of movements is created. Our family sports group did just this and successfully demonstrated a turn with games and gymnastics using hoops at the REHA '91 (Rehabilitation Fair 1991) in Düsseldorf.

Pony and Cart

Rules of the Game:

A grown-up and a child together pick up a hoop. First of all the child acts as the pony with the grown-up holding the hoop round its waist running behind as the cart. There are several songs or music which can be used to accompany this game. After a certain time the roles are changed over and the grown-up becomes the pony and the child the cart.

Variations:

* The pony runs, trots, gallops ...
* The cart moves in different directions round the hall.

Carriage and Pair

Rules of the Game:

Two horses, two hoops and two coachmen turn into a carriage and pair and trot together round the hall.

Variations:

* The horses run, trot, gallop ...
* The carriage moves in different directions round the hall.
* The 'horses' changeover to be the 'carriage'.
* Four 'horses' and then you have a four-in-hand.

Obstacle Course

Rules of the Game:

The hoops are laid down on the ground and people run round them.

Variations:

* Run past as many hoops as possible.
* Use other objects as obstacles.
* When the music stops: stand in pairs inside the hoop, or e.g., drive the wheelchair onto the mat.

Steeplechase

Rules of the Game:
The child holds the hoop horizontally about six inches to one foot off the ground. The grown-up has to jump in and out of the hoop.

Variations:
- Hold the hoop higher.
- Change over positions.
- Hold the hoop vertically.

Gymnastics with the Hoops

Rules of the Game:
From the wide selection of possibilities to devise gymnastics for use with hoops, here are a few examples for partners – for grown-ups and children, disabled with able bodied. It is recommended that the music accompanying is changed from a swinging to rapid beat music alternately.

Variations:
- Swinging: both partners catch hold of the hoop and swing it between them backwards and forwards.
- Swinging can be increased so that the hoop goes over in a circle while at the same time the partners turn round.
- Upper body backwards and forwards:
  - Both partners sit down opposite each other with their legs outstretched and grab hold of the hoop. They now move the hoop backwards and forwards alternately. They can also roll their upper body round in unison.
- Climbing through the hoop:
  - Both partners climb through the hoop at the same time.
- Twisting:
  - One of the partners twists the hoop round on the spot. As long as the hoop is twisting both of them run round the hoop and have to catch it just before it drops down flat on the floor.
- Rolling the hoop and jumping:
  - One of the partners rolls the hoop along while the other runs alongside and tries to jump through the rolling hoop.

Gymnastics and Relaxation

(see chapter B.II.2)

5.2   Dancing

Simple dances are very popular in family sport with disabled people. They give all the participants the opportunity to carry out something jointly. Spurred on by the music, which gives it a clearer meaning, these exercises can be made to work very successfully. Here is a short summary of some of these dances:

"I'm a Little Teddy Bear"

Rules of the Game:

All stand round in a circle and sing. One of the children circles round the group to the music and chooses a partner to dance with. The two of them dance together. Then two children circle around and do the same, then four and so on until all the children have turned into 'Little Teddy Bears'. The text of the song is:

> "Teddy bear, teddy bear, turn around,
> Teddy bear, teddy bear, touch the ground.
> Teddy bear, teddy bear, show your dirty shoe,
> Teddy bear, teddy bear, that will do.
>
> Teddy bear, teddy bear, climb upstairs,
> Teddy bear, teddy bear, say your prayers.
> Teddy bear, teddy bear, turn off the light.
> Teddy bear, teddy bear say goodnight."

Stepping over Stepping Stones

(see chapter B.I.3.2)

Dancing in Circles

Rules of the Game:

Dance around in circles to simple and clearly structured music: e.g.:

> "Can you walk on two legs, two legs, two legs?
> Can you walk on two legs, round and round and round?
> I can walk on two legs, two legs, two legs,
> I can walk on two legs, round and round and round
>
> Can you hop on one leg? etc
> Can you wave with one hand? etc
> Can you wave with two hands? etc"

Alternative:

> "8 steps in a circle to the right
> 8 steps in a circle to the left
> 4 steps to the centre
> 4 steps back
> 8 x clap your hands or stamp your feet" – repeat

Polonaise

Rules of the Game:
All dance the polonaise together to simple marching music:

- In twos together in a circle.
- In fours together in a circle, then through the middle of each other and split off into pairs.
- Dance through an archway and so on.

Dancing down the Path

Rules of the Game:
All the sports group participants form a path about 2-3 m wide down the hall. In pairs people dance down the path to a swinging musical rhythm. Everybody standing in the path has to copy the movements of those dancing down the path, but in such a distorted manner that quite comical movements are formed.

---

1   The male form is used in the games for simplification. The female form is always meant as well.
2   'Völker-Ball' is a popular game in Germany. Game for two teams where the object is to hit an opponent with a ball and thus put him out of the game.
3   Compare KIPHARD 1979, 1983, 1989; IRMSCHER 1980, 1981; ZIMMER 1987 inter alia.
4   The bell ball is a ball with a bell fixed inside.
5   A trolley board is any equipment that consists of a board fitted with wheels or castors underneath.

II. Integrated Family Sport

Part 2: Alternatives

While in the first part the emphasis was on movement, sports and games for the whole family, this part deals with different heterogeneous target groups.

Small children, disabled children, youths, grown-ups, fathers, mothers and even grandparents all arrive with different interests, expectations and requirements. This means that at least one part of the sports session must take these interests into consideration. In the long-term there is a danger that families will only engage themselves in family sport, leaving individual family members only partially able to fulfil their own requirements and expectations.

In this way, differentiation of integration, which is understood as the reciprocal dependence of the development of the personality and social integration (see RHEKER 1989a, 122), can only gain a chance of realisation by carrying out family sport with disabled and able bodied people.

By offering a variety for the different target groups, which is of importance next to joint activities available to the whole family, the individual has room to be able to develop himself and achieve his own concept and idea for sports and games he wishes to undertake.

In our family sport sessions sometimes there are about 20 families taking part. Because of the size of the group it is therefore very necessary to account for all. This is further facilitated by the availability of a large three-sectioned exercise hall with an additional multi-gym.

This is also the reason why we divide the middle part of each sports session into three or four smaller groups:
1. A group for disabled and younger able bodied children
2. A parent's group
3. A group for disabled youths and able bodied older children
4. A crawler group for the very young children and a few parents.

Contents

1. Games and Sport for the Disabled and Younger Able Bodied Children

This target group has three choices, which are quite easily switched from one to the other:

1. Trampoline
2. Obstacle courses and adventure games
3. Games to further awareness of the body, environment, equipment and society.

1.1 Trampoline

Exercises on the trampoline give the effect and feeling of flying and weightlessness to many children and youths who have tried it out. The particular characteristics of this equipment make it very suitable for exercises and the furtherance of various basic motor activities such as:

- Self-confidence and trust in others
- Sense of responsibility
- The joy of movement
- Preparedness to take risks
- Concentration
- Self-awareness
- Sensory motor adaptability
- Rhythm
- Sense of balance
- Posture building
- Position sense
- Orientation
- Co-ordination
- Skills
- Endurance
- Jumping strength

There is no other piece of equipment, which positively influences the development of the functions balance, ability to co-ordinate and motor activity capability, as much as the programmed use of the trampoline. The bouncing feeling and the 'ability to fly' is very appealing and full of fun for children of all ages, irrespective of whether they are disabled or able bodied. The characteristic of challenge is therefore rated highly by children using it. At the same time it gives a very direct sense of achievement.

Exercises range from basic ones, where the bounce of the trampoline is first experienced and which serves as a good introduction for disabled children, then progress on to learning to do little jumps, which even little children and also the disabled can manage to control. These basic exercises e.g., landing on the stomach and bouncing up and over on to the back, are very suitable for relaxation and loosening up exercises.

The Basics of Using the Trampoline

So that best use can be made of the trampoline, the exercise supervisor must have a good knowledge of the equipment as well as the safety rules and the various uses it can be put to, and movements that can be carried out on it.

The trampoline should only be used under supervision. Where possible no more than four people should be involved in the setting up and packing up of the equipment, providing they have sufficient strength to do this. If there are too many helpers involved, there is a danger that no one will feel responsible for his actions and, anyway, they may all get in each other's way, risking even more danger. All people helping must work in unison with the others. Furthermore, in order to ensure that possible faults can be recognised in advance, before the equipment is set up, it must be checked over to establish that all the pieces are in a good condition (especially the elevating stands). The final responsibility lies with the exercise supervisor.

Here a few basic tips about setting up and packing up the trampoline. The setting up must be carried out carefully to ensure that accidents and injury are eliminated as far as possible. When the equipment is set up, it must be checked before anyone starts bouncing on it.

The trampoline must be boxed off and soft mats laid down on each of its ends to heighten the safety factor as far as possible. On each side soft mats or matting must also be laid down. In order to facilitate climbing on and off the equipment, position a small crate or box steps at one side.

Behaviour on the trampoline: the trampoline must not be used unsupervised or without safety catchers standing in position.

Where the children are particularly nervous for the first time, or in the case of the disabled, they should be broken into their first attempts at jumping by learning the bouncing feeling, and then progress step-by-step, gradually moving on to jumping.

The exercise challenges and speed of the methodical approach must keep pace always with the individual performance reached by each child and not overstep it.

There should always be 2-3 grown-ups positioned along the side of the equipment as safety personnel. Jumpers must dismount from the equipment using the steps provided at one end of the trampoline (never jump off the trampoline!)

Trampoline Jumping

Picture 10:
The trampoline is an exciting
piece of equipment and can
be used to achieve several
objectives.

• **Experiencing**
  the Basics through to
  Jumping

Exercises to Learn the Bounce on the Trampoline ⎯⎯⎯⎯⎯⎯⎯⎯⎯
• Up to three children lie down on their backs on the trampoline. The others sit on the
  side and gently bounce the children lying down, up and down.
• As above but the children lie on their stomachs or on their sides.
• As above but sitting down or kneeling.

The First Movements on the Trampoline ⎯⎯⎯⎯⎯⎯⎯⎯⎯
We can inform ourselves about the state of development of a young child's motor
activity.
• Roll sideways (head over heels) over several trampolines which have been
  positioned together.
• 'Crawling' on all fours over the trampoline.
  - Ambling gait (right hand and right knee together).

- Arms and knees diagonally.
- Hopping like a frog.
• Other ways of 'crawling': e.g., backwards etc.
• Moving over the trampoline with the help of a partner. First of all the partner holds both hands and later only one hand.
• The partner leads the other over various different parts of the trampoline: across the middle, along the side, from corner to corner, across the side wires.
• These exercises can be carried out also with the eyes closed.
• The partner varies the speed he also leads the other.
• Walk raising the knees up high.
• Vary the way of moving: small steps, backwards, sideways, move like different animals (camel, frog ...).

Changing over from Bouncing to Jumping

The exercise supervisor (acting as the partner) holds the child by both hands. The child lets itself be bounced as the supervisor moves the surface of the trampoline up and down by giving it a slight impulse.

• As above, but the child copies the impulse and increases the up and down movement itself. The child's feet stay firmly on the trampoline's surface.
• The bouncing movement is now increased so that the heels begin to lift off. The balls of the feet and toes stay on the surface of the trampoline.
• By bouncing more the feet lift off completely.
• Step-by-step the partner begins to drop out:
    - Both hands holding.
    - Only holding with one hand.
    - One hand holds on lightly.
    - When the child starts to bounce itself the partner continues to watch safety aspects.
    – Increase the bouncing until the jumping stage is reached.

The Foot Jump

To learn the foot jump, the criteria of the technicalities have to be practised time and time again to perfect it:
• Plant the feet flat on the surface and stretch up onto the toes.
• Jump on the centre point of the trampoline.
• Take up swinging the arms in rhythm.
• Close the legs when in the air, and on landing open them slightly.
• Stiffen up the body.

• **Further Basic Jumps:**
- Do a foot jump with a 1/4 and 1/2 screw turn / – squatting jump/ – straddle vault jump/ – jumping doing the splits/ – jack-knife jump/ – sitting jump (first of all with assistance, later without)/ – sitting jump, 1/2 screw turn, jumping up from this position to the standing position/ – sitting jump, 1/2 screw turn back down into the sitting position – different combinations of the basic jumping forms.

• **Trampoline Jumping and the Training of the Perceptive Senses without Additional Equipment**

Being Bounced
The child lies on the trampoline and lets itself be bounced. Which side is being bounced greater?

Variation:
• Do this in different positions: on the back, on the stomach, on the side, sitting.

Awareness
The child lies on the trampoline with its eyes closed. Another child moves about on the trampoline. The child lying down has to point out exactly where the other child is.

Variation:
• The second child walks, creeps, hops ...

Moving on the Trampoline
The child is lead over various parts of the trampoline.

Variation:
• With its eyes closed.

With closed eyes the child has to find the middle point in the trampoline by walking to it or running, or hopping.

Calling the Jumps
Variations:
• Stop.
• Crouch, straddle vault, jack-knife, jumping the splits.
• Half screw turn, jumping in the sitting position.

- Jumping and recognising signs given by the exercise supervisor standing at the end of the trampoline: hand signs, number of fingers held up, coloured handkerchiefs ...
- Jumping when shown certain signs: triangle, square ...
- Matching the jumps to those of the partner.

Bobsleigh

3-6 children sit down all behind each other. They play bobsleigh as they go through different curves and downhill stretches. People standing around bounce the sides of the trampoline up and down.

'Ox on the Hill'

The game 'Ox on the Hill' can also be played on the trampoline.

- **Trampoline Jumping and the Training of the Perceptive Senses with Additional Equipment**

Trampoline and Rhythm/Music

Bounce on the trampoline and/or jump to the music e.g., accompaniment from a tambourine, maracas ...
Variation:
- Adopting various positions: lying on the stomach, back, side, sitting, standing.

Move around in small groups to the music.
Variation: • As above.

Jumping on the trampoline to music.
Variation: • Alone, in twos.

Trampoline and Ropes

Balance on a rope laid down on the trampoline.
Variations:
- With or without the help of a partner.
- With eyes closed.
- The rope is placed on different parts of the trampoline.

Balance on different ropes that have been laid out in various patterns on the trampoline.
Variation: • As above.

4-8 ropes are laid out on the trampoline forming different sized circles. Everyone has to walk or hop from one to the other.

Variations:
- As above.
- *Imagine you are a tree and have to be uprooted and planted in another plot.

Jumping over Ropes

1-3 ropes are laid out across the trampoline. You have to run over them or jump over them.

Variations:
- The ropes are held at different heights.
- Jump like the game of jumping through the skipping rope.
- Jump over a rope (held low down), touch a rope held up high.

Picking Sweets

Sweets or coloured pieces of paper are fixed to a rope that is held up high. You have to pick them off the rope as you bounce up high.

Variation: • Bite into apples or take a sniff of a 'smelly sack'.

Bamboo Twist

Two ropes are held by people standing who pull the ropes apart and bring them back together again. Someone jumps up and down to the same rhythm – either with legs apart or closed together.

Jumping with the Rope on the Trampoline

Jumping on the trampoline using the rope.

Variations:
- Swinging the rope forwards, backwards.
- Swing the rope over twice.
- Jumping on different parts of the trampoline.
- Double up the rope and jump over it.
- Jumping on one leg.

Jumping on the Trampoline with a Long Rope

Two people stand, one at each end on the mat by the trampoline, and swing a long rope. One person jumps over the rope as it swings.

Variation: • Two or more people jumping.

• Trampoline and Little Boxes

Playing Ships

A child sits in an upturned small box. Everyone standing around gently shakes the box to give the effect of waves in the sea. At the same time a story can be related which changes the rhythm from a storm through gentle waves to an absolute still.

The Riding Game

Somebody sits on a box, which is placed on the trampoline. The people standing around bounce the surface of the trampoline up and down until the person is 'riding' the box like a horse.

The Big Dipper

Two to four people sit on two small boxes, which are lined up behind each other on the trampoline. The people standing around now begin to bounce them as if they were on the 'Big Dipper'. The 'riders' can throw their weight to the left and go round a left banking and then to the right to negotiate a right banking. When going uphill they all lean backwards and the opposite when they are going downhill.

Variations:
• Go through different curves and uphill, downhill, different combinations.
• Bumpy stretches: the people doing the bouncing make violent up and down movements.

The Magic Carpet

A person sits on a mat lying on the trampoline. This is bounced up and down until the carpet is 'flying'.

Variations:
• Dependent on the bouncing movements and impulses, the carpet 'flies' at different heights.
• Lying down on the mat.
• Two people on the magic carpet.

• The Trampoline and Sheets

The combination of the trampoline and a sheet or parachute affords many new and unusual experiences for the topic awareness and movement.

Moving under the Sheet on the Trampoline

One to six children lie under a sheet stretched out on the trampoline and are bounced up and down gently.

Variations:
- The sheet lies on top of the children.
- The sheet is held just a little off the children.
- Changeover from gentle bouncing to more violent bouncing.
- Lie in different positions under the sheet.

Jumping in all Weathers

Four people standing on the corners of the trampoline hold the sheet up high. The sheet represents the sky and one to four children bounce or jump up and down under it. First of all the sheet is held up high to represent a clear bright sky. Then the wind gets up and the sheet is moved up and down to represent the clouds. The children can now bounce up into the clouds. The wind can now be turned into a storm or even into a thunderstorm or a hurricane by moving the sheet more violently while at the same time bringing the sheet down onto the children.

Igloo on the Trampoline

On the trampoline, four to six people, sit on the edge of a sheet or parachute and hold it above themselves with their hands to form an igloo. People standing round the trampoline now bounce the 'igloo inhabitants' up and down.

Variations:
- The shape of the igloo can be changed by some of the 'inhabitants' standing up to make it taller.
- The 'igloo inhabitants' do a dance in their tent.

Moving around on the Sheet and the Trampoline

The sheet is laid loosely on the trampoline. One to four people now move around on the sheet, crawling, walking or hopping. When one person (at a time) jumps up and down, waves appear in the sheet on the trampoline.

Variations:
- The sheet is held down and stretched flat by the people standing around the trampoline.
- Switch between having the sheet stretched out flat and being held loosely.
- Do the exercise to music.

• The Trampoline and the Pedal-vehicle

Using the pedal-vehicle on the trampoline requires special co-ordination powers. This starts off by having a partner assist. This assistance can be gradually dropped off until the rider is going on his own.

Variations:
- Use the rehabilitation pedal-vehicle.
- Use a long chassis pedal-vehicle and do it in pairs or threes.
- The two-seater pedal-vehicle follows someone around by virtue of that person's bouncing movements. The pedal-vehicle reacts like an obedient dog following on behind that hops when bounced.

• The Trampoline and Other Equipment

The Trampoline and the Ball

While bouncing and jumping catch a sorbo rubber ball, which is thrown from the end of the trampoline, and throw it back.

The Trampoline and a Sack

Bounce up and down on the trampoline standing in a sack.

Variation: • While jumping pull the sack off.

1.2 Obstacle Courses and Adventure Games

By doing obstacle courses and adventure games, children learn to exercise and experience several motor activities. They should be able to have fun doing this as well as try out movements and have a good time together with others etc.

Obstacles should open up a multitude of different ways of moving. The equipment should be so laid out to create the possibility to exercise the following motor activities and skills: climbing, swinging, hanging by the hands, rolling, balancing.

One way of accomplishing all these is already available using the normal equipment found in the gymnasium.

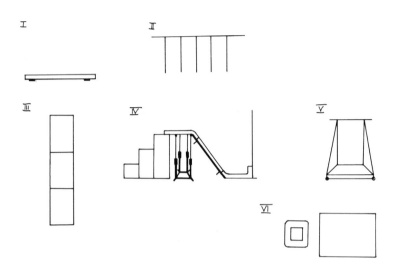

Diagram 7: An example of an obstacle course[1]

Balancing

Benches, upturned balancing bars and low balancing rails.

Variations:
- Different width to balance on.
- Balancing on level objects as well as slopes.

Swinging and Climbing

Boxes and ropes laid out so that you can swing, using the rope, from one to another.

Climbing, Rolling and Other Activities on the Slope

Adjust the vaulting horse to its highest extremity. On one side of it hook three benches onto the bar. Lay on these some thick matting to form the slope area. Lay some matting on the top to form the pedestal. On the other side build up boxes to form steps to climb up.

The Large Swing

Construct a base using hanging ropes and beams through the rings on the end of the ropes, so that a mattress and/or an area of matting can be laid over it. This then forms a large swing for the children to swing and see-saw on.

Picture 11: The swing is very popular.

The Little Springboard and Soft Matting

(Assistance when using this is absolutely necessary!)

1.3 Games to Further Awareness of the Body, Environment, Equipment and Society

Games to further awareness of the body, environment, equipment and society were already introduced in chapter B, I.4. A summary of all the games with this objective can be found in the Games - Data Bank.

2. Games for the Parents

Parents must be given the chance, during this part of the sports session, to have at least one opportunity to do something towards improving their health, and to be able to develop their own interest in leisure activities as well as do things with other parents and come into contact with them, to have a 'natter' and broaden the contact – without having to worry about their children.

Parents quite often choose the following activities which take place in a separate part of the gymnasium:
- Leisure games such as shuttlecock/badminton, 'Völker-Ball', ball over the rope, soccer or hockey.
- Various gymnastics.
- Dancing.

The following games and exercise forms are usually the most popular with the parents:

2.1   Leisure Games and Activities

Shuttlecock/Badminton
This is a very popular game that can be played, not only as a leisure activity, but also as a competitive game.

Variations:
- Play it with a balloon.
- Keep the shuttlecock up in the air as long as possible.
- Play together.
- Play with the opposite hand to the normal one.
- Play doubles.
- Play to the official rules.
- Play the game in a wheelchair.

Further Leisure Games
- Ball over the rope.
- Play 'Völker-Ball'.
- Play indoor hockey or soccer.

2.2   Gymnastics

Gymnastics should provide relaxation and an outlet from everyday burdens as well as an opportunity to improve general fitness. Parents generally prefer the following forms of gymnastics: general fitness gymnastics (to music), aerobics, spinal cord exercises and stretching.

2.3   Relaxation Exercises

Progressive Relaxation ━━━━━━━━━━━━━━━━━━━━━━━━━━━━━━━━━━━━

The method of progressive relaxation designed by JACOBSON[2] is particularly effective and popular. This technique involves creating an intensive feeling in the muscles by flexing the muscular structure. This results in a centralised feeling of relaxation with an accompanying inner relaxation and calming effect. Before describing the exercises for progressive relaxation here are a few tips:

- Wear comfortable warm clothing: warm socks, no shoes, no restrictions such as a belt
- Soft surfaces (blankets, mats ...).
- A quiet softly lit room (close the eyes).
- Start gently when exercising children; start with short sessions, later longer; move from flexing the whole body to flexing various body parts (slowly flex to different degrees).
- Verbal instructions when exercising should be given in a quiet, slow and soothing manner. They should complement the relaxation exercises.

As an example, verbal instructions should be like this:
> "Make a fist, clench it tightly,
> Try to feel the tension,
> And now, relax ...
> All is calm, nothing moves ...
> I can feel my hand getting warm ...
> I can feel my arm getting heavy ..."

While doing the progressive relaxation exercises, specific groups of muscles are tensed and held for a certain length of time. Then there follows an intensive period of relaxation before the same group of muscles are tensed again. The following sequence of exercises have proved useful:

Upper extremities:
1.	Right fist	2x
2.	Left fist	2x
3.	Both fists	1x
4.	Right bicep (bend the arm)	2x
5.	Left bicep	2x
6.	Both biceps	1x
7.	Pull the shoulders up	2x
8.	Tuck the head back into the shoulders	2x
9.	Move the head to the left/right side	2x
10.	Drop the chin onto the chest	2x

Head: All exercises   2x
1.	Push the forehead upwards
2.	Push the forehead downwards
3.	Squeeze the eyes together
4.	Rumple up the nose
5.	Clench the teeth together
6.	Thrust the tongue under the gums
7.	Pout the lips forward

Bottom:
1.	Breathe in deeply and hold your breath	2x
2.	Push the tummy out	2x
3.	Pull the tummy in	2x
4.	Push the tummy out and pull it in abruptly	1x
5.	Push your spine down flat on the ground	2x

Lower extremities:
1.	Tighten the thigh and bottom muscles	2x
2.	Flex the feet up towards the shinbone	2x
3.	Flex the toes up and down	2x

The end of the exercise session, during which some of the participants may well fall asleep, must be conducted quietly and gently. Gentle breathing in and out exercises follow and then steadily stretch the body completely, and only after this, stand up slowly.

The relaxation exercises can be adapted, dependent on the type of group exercising. For children the exercises should start with exercises involving the whole of the body and then move onto differing degrees of tensing parts of the body and different small muscle groups. The following games can be used as an **introduction for children to relaxation exercises and techniques:**

The Lilo
A child lies on its back on a mat. The child plays the part of a lilo-mattress. Another child plays the role of someone trying to pump up the lilo (= the child's body) – until all the pockets (= muscles) in the mattress are pumped up. The child now pulls the "stopper" out and the lilo flops down again.

Blow-up Rubber Animals
In this game a child plays the role of a blow-up rubber animal toy in which various of its parts can be blown-up separately. Thus the right leg can be blown-up first (tighten up the muscles in the right leg) and then have the air let out again, or, blow-up (flex or tension) another part of the body.

2.4   Dancing
The ladies group will often come forward to request that a special dance or other can be practised for a particular occasion such as a carnival demonstration or a jubilee event. This can be done with a lot of fun and enjoyment until it is ready for the occasion.

Picture 12: A simple circular dance.

3.   Games for Disabled Youths and Older Able Bodied Children

Participants in this group often want to have a good workout in one part of the sports session in order to try out and exercise specific motor activities or just simply train. This session is therefore designed for them. Under the supervision of the exercise leader the participant's individual interests can be accommodated. Some of the following games can be used:

3.1   Team Games for a Workout

Indoor Hockey

Rules of the Game:
Both teams try to score a goal using a puck and plastic toy hockey sticks. The goal can be made from an upturned box, whereby the slot in the middle of the base is where the puck has to pass through to score a goal. Team strength: 3-6 players.

Variation:
• Create a 'shooting circle' from which the shot has to be made.

Indoor Football

Rules of the Game:
Play using simplified rules that are adjusted according to target group.

Basketball

Rules of the Game:
Play using simplified rules: e.g., hitting the backboard = one point; hitting the centre of the backboard = two points; scoring a basket = three points. The game can also be played using wheelchairs.

Variation:
• The basketball rules can be adjusted in stages; two steps rule; fouls rules etc

The Multi-goal Game

Rules of the Game:
Four or more goals are erected on the playing area e.g., by using cones or boxes. Two teams try to score a goal by hitting them with a ball, so that the ball is caught or trapped behind the cone by a player on the same side.

Variation:
- Play the game with a handball according to handball rules.
- Running with the ball is not allowed.
- Play the game with a basketball according to basketball rules.
- Play the game with a hockey ball according to hockey rules.
- Play the game with a football according to the rules of soccer.

The Dice Game

Rules of the Game:

Two soft mats are laid out on the ground as goals. Two teams play soccer with a large polystyrene dice. If the dice lands on the mat the team scores the number of dots on the dice showing uppermost as goals or points.

Variations:
- Play the game with a sorbo-rubber ball according to handball or basketball rules.
- Play the game with a normal handball, football or basketball. When a goal is scored throw the dice to decide how many points are scored.

'Shove'

Rules of the Game:

Two people stand opposite each other about 1m apart and hold their hands at chest height. Each tries to unbalance the other.

Variations:
- Play as a group – two groups stand with their backs to each other. Each group links arms. Each group tries to 'shove' the other group away.

'Tug'

Rules of the Game:

Two players stand in front of each other and grasp each other by the right hand. Each tries now to tug the other over to his side.

Variation: • Use the left hands.

Tug-of-war without a Rope

Rules of the Game:

Two people play tug-of-war with an imaginary rope. Each person imagines they really have a rope in their hands i.e., thickness and texture. As much energy can be expended playing this game as with a real rope.

Variation:
- Two groups, each of 3-10 players, line up against each other so that the first person in the group catches hold of the hand of the opposing team. The other players in each team grasp each other round the waist. The teams now tug each other like the tug-of-war.

Hopping Snakes
Rules of the Game:
Form two teams, each of 5-12 players. Each team member lines up behind the next. Each person behind lays his left hand on the front-man's shoulder and holds up the left foot of the man in front using his right hand. The team now hops along over a specific distance without the snake breaking up.

Variations:
- Hop down a straight course.
- Hop on the left leg.
- Hop round a turning point and hop back to the start.
- Slalom.
- Hop backwards.

'Wobbly Snakes'
Rules of the Game:
Form two teams, each of 5-12 players. Each team's players form a 'wobbly snake' by each person grasping the left hand of the man in front with his right hand, and sticking his left hand through his own legs to the man behind. The idea is now to cover a certain distance e.g., the length of the gymnasium, without anyone loosing his grip.

Variations:
- Cover a straight course (e.g., the length of the basketball field).
- Running round a turning point and back to the start.
- Slalom.
- Go over obstacles (boxes, benches ...).

Fireman's Lift
Rules of the Game:
Form between 3-10 teams each of 5-10 players. Members of each team line up behind each other. The first man carries the second over a specific distance (e.g., fireman's lift). The second man runs back to the start and carries the third man to the end and so on until the last man has been carried.

Variations:
*   Carried out as a slalom relay.
*   Go over various surfaces – soft mats, hard mats ...
*   In water: the partner is pulled or pushed along in the floating position.

'Mat Sailing'

Rules of the Game:
Teams of six people each have to try to move a thick soft mat over to the other side of the gymnasium with the least number of attempts – the mat can only be 'sailed' along by jumping onto it to move it. A giant dice is thrown to determine how many people can jump on the mat at any one time.

Variations:
     • Only one person at a time can jump on the mat to sail it.
     • Two or three ... players can jump and 'sail'.
     • Each team throws its own dice.
     • A supervisor throws the dice for all teams.

3.2   Games of Skill with Equipment

Children and youths in this group often like to have the opportunity to simply try out a new skill or trick with special equipment (trolley board, pedal-vehicle, skateboard, wheelchair: ideas for games see chapter B.I.4.2 and chapter B.V).

3.3   Games with the Racquet and the Bat

Some children and youths have quite specific ideas of particular games they want to play such as table tennis, badminton/shuttlecock.

Sometimes youths wish to use this part of the sports session to follow their own individual wishes. For example the high-jump can be practiced in one part of the gymnasium whilst table tennis is being played in another.

4. Games for Infant Groups

We were able to ascertain that there was a pleasing tendency that parents, with children as young as 1-6 years old, also sought to visit the family sports groups. As a result we included a section for this target group. In the University/Polytechnic (of Paderborn), besides the multi-roomed main gymnasium, there is an additional gymnasium room that we have put to use for this parent's group with their 'kiddies'. Here the parents and their little charges can carry on their own programme of little games, singing, dancing and exercises under the direction of a trained supervisor and one of the mothers, without the disturbing influence of external diversions.

Here the little children get their first opportunity of taking their first steps without parents overseeing what they are doing. Similarly the parents get the opportunity to have some freedom of activity, whether it be to carry out sport or play together with other parents; dancing or simply to have a conversation.

In this crawler group there are three main points of emphasis:
- Joining hands games in a circle, singing games or finger games.
- Playing with the aid of equipment.
- Dances.

4.1 Games in the Circle, Singing and Games with the Fingers

All Clap Hands

All the children stand around in a circle with one child sitting in the middle and they sing:

> *"We'll all clap hands*
> *We'll all clap hands together,*
> *We'll all clap hands together,*
> *We'll all clap hands together,*
> *As children like to do.*
>
> *We'll all stand up together etc*
>
> *We'll all sit down together etc*
>
> *We'll all jump together etc."*

The child in the middle stands up and runs to one of the children in the circle who now has to go to be in the middle.

Looby Loo

All the children stand round in a circle and sing the song acting out words as far as possible.

> *"Here we go Looby Loo*
> *Here we go Looby Light*
> *Here we go Looby Loo*
> *All on a Saturday night*
>
> *You put your right foot in*
> *You put your foot out*
> *You shake it a little, a little*
> *And turn yourself about*
>
> *You put your left foot in, etc*
>
> *You put your right hand in, etc*
>
> *You put your left hand in, etc*
>
> *You put your whole self in, etc."*

Alternative songs follow:

1. *"Wind the bobbin up,*
    (roll fists round each other)

    Wind the bobbin up,

    Pull, pull, clap, clap, clap:
    (pull fists apart as though pulling elastic, then clap)

    Point to the ceiling,
    (do the actions as they are mentioned)

    Point to the floor,

    Point to the window,

    Point to the door,
    Clap your hands together,

    One, two, three,

    Put your hands upon your knees."

2.   *"You twiddle your thumbs and clap your hands,*
        And then you stamp your feet.
        You turn to the left, you turn to the right,
        You make your fingers meet.
        You make a bridge, you make an arch,
        You give another clap.
        You wave your hands, you fold your hands,
        Then lay them in your lap."

Standing in a circle – do the actions above as they are mentioned.

"I Sent a Letter to My Love"

All the children except one sit down in a circle. The odd one runs round the outside of the ring while the song is sung and drops a handkerchief behind one of the seated children. The chosen child picks the handkerchief up and tries to catch the other child before he/she reaches the empty space.

        "I sent a letter to my love
        And on the way I dropped it;
        One of you has picked it up
        And put it in your pocket."

If the child is not caught the new child becomes the one who runs round and drops the handkerchief.

Games with the Fingers

These are very suitable games for the improvement or the development of eye-hand co-ordination.

"This Little Pig Went to Market"

All sit round in a circle and follow the actions of the supervisor.

   "This little pig went to market
   (the supervisor (S) grabs hold of his thumb and wobbles it to and fro)
   This little pig stayed at home
   (S grabs hold of his forefinger and wiggles it round)
   This little pig had roast beef
   (S grabs hold of his middle finger and wiggles it around)
   This little pig had none
   (S grabs hold of the next finger and holds it still)

And this little pig said, "Wee, wee, wee"
(S holds his little finger and holds it still)
All the way home"
(Each child turns to the one on his right and runs his hand over the shoulders and tickles him under the arms.)

Teddy Bear

The children sit in pairs. The supervisor is also paired off with one of the children. One of the partners does the following actions to the other while repeating the verses:

"Round and round the garden (*One of them runs his forefinger in a circle*
went the teddy bear, (*on the palm of the other child's hand*)
1 step, 2 steps, and tickly under there (*Move the finger up the arm to tickle*)

Round and round the hay stack
went a little mouse (*ditto & changeover between partners*)
1 step, 2 step in his little house.

Slowly, slowly, very slowly
creeps the garden snail
Slowly, slowly, very slowly (*ditto & changeover between partners*)
up the wooden rail

Quickly, Quickly
runs the little mouse
Quickly, quickly (*ditto & changeover between partners*)
runs the little mouse
round about the house."

The Finger Family

"This is the father short and stout,
This is the mother with children all about
This is the brother tall you see
This is the sister with a dolly on her knee
This is the baby sure to grow
And here is the family all in a row."

Start with the thumb pointing to all fingers in turn and on the last line hold all the fingers up outstretched.

"Knock at the Door"

"Knock at the door,	*(pretend to knock on the forehead)*
Pull the bell,	*(lightly pull a lock of hair)*
Lift the latch,	*(lightly pinch the nose)*
And walk in	*(pretend to put your fingers on his mouth.)"*

"Here We Go round the Mulberry Bush"

All the children form a circle and when they sing the first verse (the chorus) they skip around in a circle. When singing the other verses, with the chorus in between, they stand still, face inwards and act out the words.

Chorus

"Here we go round the mulberry bush
the mulberry bush, the mulberry bush
here we go round the mulberry bush, on a cold and frosty morning."

"This is the way we wash our face, wash our face, wash our face etc
This is the way we comb our hair etc
This is the way we brush our teeth etc."

Final chorus

"Do your ears hang low? Do they wobble to and fro?
Can you tie them in a knot? Can you tie them in a bow?
Can you toss them over your shoulder like a regimental soldier?
Do your ears hang low?"

"London Bridge Is Falling down, Falling down, Falling down"

This game can be played just as a dance but if the ideas of the children are solicited, objects can be used to represent some of the actions in the words.

Chorus

"London Bridge is falling down, Falling down, Falling down
London Bridge is falling down, Falling down, Falling down
My fair lady"

Build it up with iron bars, etc

Iron bars will bend and bow, etc

Build it up with pins and needles, etc

Pins and needles will rust and bend, etc

Build it up with gold and silver, etc

Gold and silver I have not got, etc

Here's a prisoner I have got, etc

What's the prisoner done to you, etc

Stole my watch and broke my chain, etc

What'll you take to set him free, etc

One hundred pounds will set him free, etc

One hundred pounds we have not got, etc

Then off to prison he must go, etc

*"Ring a Ring o'Roses"*_____

All form a circle and dance around.

> *"Ring a ring o'roses,*
> *A pocket full of posies,*
> *A-tishoo, a-tishoo,*
> *We all fall down.*   *(Everyone falls down on the ground in a heap)*

> *The king has sent his daughter*
> *To fetch a pail of water,*
> *A-tishoo, a-tishoo,*
> *We all fall down."*   *(ditto)*

4.2   Games with Equipment

Using different pieces of equipment, children can learn their characteristics and how to use them to play and do movements with, and to gain experience trying them out. In this way they can increase their knowledge about the environment and equipment, and collect valuable information to improve their own ability to move about.

For this target group – the pre-school age – the following, in all sizes and colours, are suitable; hoops, little ropes, sheets, gymnastic equipment (mats, little boxes), balancing benches, rice bags.

Picture 13: Parents and little children can gain a lot of experience in the crawler group.

• Balls

Game possibilities with different balls (tennis balls, different coloured gymnastic balls, balloons):
*   Throwing, rolling, catching.
*   Putting or throwing them into or at a target (little boxes).
*   Striking (with the hand).
*   Sorting the balls by colours.
*   Sorting the balls by weight or size.
*   Rolling the ball to someone/handing from one to another/throwing at each other.
*   Keeping baskets filled.
*   Keeping your play area clear.
*   Relay races with balls.
*   Hunting ball games (see Ball Games in the Data Bank).

• Hoops

Try out game possibilities with hoops and adopt games devised by the children such as:
*   Rolling hoops.
*   Laying the hoops on the ground and jumping in and out of them.
*   Twisting hoops.
*   Hula hoop.
*   Holding the hoops and playing cars running around the hall.
*   Further games (see chapter B.I.5.1).

Room to Let

Rules of the Game:
Each child lays its hoop down somewhere in the room. The hoops represent houses or rooms. One hoop is taken away. The children run round amongst the rooms. On a signal each child tries to occupy one of the rooms. One of the children will be left over who has to shout out "room to let", whereupon everyone leaves their hoops and looks for another room. Now a different child will be left over who now has to shout "room to let".

Trains

Rules of the Game:
Each child runs around the room with its hoop mimicking a railway carriage. Long trains can be built up by coupling up several carriages.

The Pony Game

Rules of the Game:
Two children hold a hoop together. One of the children is the horse while the other lets itself be pulled along in the hoop by the horse.

Variation: • Two-in-hand or a four-in-hand.

• The Balancing Bench as an Equipment for Exercising and Playing

First of all the children should be introduced to this piece of equipment by doing simple exercises and games with the bench to gain their confidence with it. The bench can then be used as an exercise equipment to improve motor activity, particularly balancing training and co-ordination abilities, and to strengthen and improve fitness. The following exercises and games can be carried out with crawler groups:

The Balancing Bench

All the children move around the hall amongst the benches to rhythmical music. When the music stops the following exercises have to be carried out:

- • Form a circle round the bench.
- • Sit down on the benches.
- • Lay down on the benches.
- • Stand on the benches.
- • Creep (or similar movements) under the benches.

Exercises on the Balancing Bench ━━━━━━━━━━━━━━━━━━

- Walk over the bench.
- Run over the bench.
- Pull oneself over the bench on the stomach.
- Lay on the bench on the back and be pulled along it or pull oneself along it.

Exercises on the Upturned Balancing Bench ━━━━━━━━━

- Balance on the narrow part with assistance from the supervisor .
- Balancing with safety measures.
- Balancing moving backwards.

Exercises on a Slanting Balancing Bench ━━━━━━━━━━

The bench is hooked into the wall-bars to form a sloping surface:

- Going up and down on all fours.
- Scrabbling up and down in the kneeling position.
- Going up and down with assistance.
- Going up and down without assistance.
- Letting a ball roll down and steering it back up – as well as other ways.

4.3   Dancing

Bingo ━━━━━━━━━━━━━━━━━━━━━━━━━━━━━━━━━━━

All the children join hands and dance around in a circle singing:

> *"A weenie little puppy, a weenie little puppy*
> *(all circle round to the right)*
> *Was sitting on the window-sill all a-floppy*
> *A weenie little puppy, a weenie little puppy*
> *(circle now to the left)*
> *Was sitting on the window-sill all a-floppy*
> *Bee / I / eN / Gee / Oh (three times)*
> *Bingo was his name*
> *(all skip round in a circle)*
> *Bee / I / eN / Gee / Oh*
> *(all move together to the middle swinging their arms up high together)*

Further dances can be found in the Data Bank under "Games Joining Hands and Singing".

1   I – a balancing bench; II – hanging ropes; III – a row of mats; IV – steps leading to a slanting surface; V – a
    large swing; VI – a springboard or trampoline.
2   JACOBSON: Progressive relaxation Chicago 1948; SCHULZ: Das autogene Training. Stuttgart 1987.

III. Integrated Family Sport

Part 3:   Projects

Not all the sports sessions for family sports groups have to be organised in the way depicted so far in this book. There are plenty of reasons for organising the whole of the sports session jointly.

For example one could choose the games for physical, equipment and social awareness as a main theme for the whole sports session. All activities would then be run along the lines of this theme and would be experienced by everyone taking part.

Moreover, once or twice a year, the family sports afternoons could take place along the same lines so that a theme is chosen and all the activities are centred on that theme. "Project sessions" such as these could have varied themes. Themes connected with particular events are very popular, such as a carnival, winter and Christmas festivities. Here are a few suggestions for project sessions that could be used on these sports afternoons.

1.   The Circus

The gymnasium can easily be turned into a circus arena without a lot of effort. A parachute, pulled up by the ring ropes or pushed up by a dividing wall, forms the tent. A large curtain can be used to divide the spectators from the "stage". Balancing benches, placed in a semicircle, can be placed in front of the curtain to mark out the 'manege' (the ring) and the 'spectator area'. A few 'props' to allow for clothing changes, dressing up and decoration must be available.

Setting the Scene

The game supervisor can start off by telling a little story:

"As you can all see the circus has come to town. The Big Top has been erected. You can already 'smell' the circus in the air. But there has been a big stroke of bad luck. Just before the first performance all the artists went down ill. What shall we do? (Pause) I've got a good idea! Let's all take on the role of the clowns, the animal trainers and the other artists and do our own circus show!"

Alternatively: all the participants in the family sports group are sitting as spectators round the manege. All of sudden the circus director comes onto the stage and begins to weep and cry loudly. He tells them why he is so sad:

"All the circus artists and the animals have run away!"

When he is asked what will happen he comes up with a splendid idea that all the 'spectators' should organise their own circus.

Workshop Groups

You can now move on to set up various workshop groups, who work up various acts or parts of the circus programme. It is recommended that the leader of the workshop groups is one of the sports supervisors or a parent, as they will be in a position to develop the ideas and stimulate the parents and the children, bringing out their hidden talents.

The suggestions made are then put together to form a programme to show in front of the others. The aim of the group work is to come up with as many ideas as possible and then to consider, all together, how these ideas can be shown. It is important to give enough leeway for all the participants – including also the little ones, the disabled and the grown-ups – so that they can put forward all their ideas for consideration. Using suitable 'props' the group's act can then be rehearsed. This concludes with the circus director announcing the programme to the audience. Workshops for the following categories can be formed: clowns, wild animals, the tightrope walker, dressage with the horses, acrobatics (juggling, strongman acts), magicians etc.

The Circus Programme

The circus director (which can be played by a child or a grown-up) assembles the programme, comes onto the stage and announces each act in turn to the audience.

THE CIRCUS AUGUSTINE PRESENTS:

1. Jugglers
2. Wild Animals
3. Clowns
4. The Tightrope Walker
5. A Dressage Show
6. Acrobats
7. The Strongman Act
8. Magicians
9. Finale

Diagram 8: The Circus Programme

The group now performs each of the acts they have rehearsed, one after the other. Anyone not actually taking part in a particular act is a spectator.

Picture 14: The acrobats show off their programme.

Picture 15: The Strongman Act – the little ones can even do this.

Our experience has been that when organising such a circus programme, everyone takes part with tremendous enthusiasm – from the youngest child through to the parents and even the grandparents. Everyone can put his own ideas into the workshop, many of which are so creative that one would never have guessed how successful they could be beforehand. The opportunity for everyone to dress up also brings many people out of their shell. Everyone can actively take part and this contributes to the success of the whole programme. Because every member of the family sports group can be included in this sort of circus programme, it always brings with it a lasting memory.

Picture 16: The tightrope walker does not have to be right up in the air.

As a finale all the actors come together in the manege and form into a big circle. Everyone dances round together to round off the project session.

2. Christmas Games

During Advent, the family sports group can use the opportunity to busy themselves with Christmas festivities as a theme during the sports afternoon. The wealth of ideas for little games has to be slightly altered to allow for the chain of events leading up to Christmas such as winter and Christmas Eve. Let us begin with a few ideas for the topic – winter:

Jack Frost

"Winter has come. Jack Frost's about. Anyone he touches also turns into a Jack Frost – they hold hands and carry on catching others."

Use the same game as 'Chain Catching' (see the Data Bank).

Icicles

Rules of the Game:
One to three catchers represent 'winter'. Anyone they touch turns into an icicle – stiff. The 'icicle' will melt (i.e., can run free again) if someone who has not yet been caught hugs the person.

Winter and Summer Fight over Their Supremacy

Rules of the Game:
Two catchers are selected. One represents 'winter' and the other 'summer'. Which one can catch the most people and beat the other one? Catching is done along the lines of the game 'Chain Catching'.

The next game couples the themes of winter and Christmas together giving the idea of moving towards Christmas Eve.

Winter – Christmas

Rules of the Game:
Two groups sit down opposite each other on the middle line of the hall about 1-2 m apart. One group is 'winter' and the other 'Christmas'. When the exercise leader calls out e.g., "winter" then the entire winter group runs away, and the Christmas group tries to catch them.

When "Christmas" is called out the same thing happens but the other way round. Compares with the game "Black and White" (see Data Bank). Closer to Christmas time the names should change and the whole scene can be embellished with a nice story. The key words appear at irregular intervals. The beginning of the story could look like this:

"Autumn creeps on. The trees begin to lose their leaves. The squirrels stock up for winter. All the trees are now bare, only the pine trees remain green. They are looking forward to Christmas ... At home the first chestnuts are being roasted. The snow is coming and all the children are looking forward to winter and Christmas."

Variations:
• Start from the sitting position, from lying on the back, on the stomach etc.
• All start waking up from winter hibernation (i.e., with closed eyes).

Father Christmas and His Reindeer

Rules of the Game:

So that Father Christmas can bring us gifts he needs his reindeer to pull his sleigh. The reindeer is in the opposite corner of the hall to Father Christmas. He has to get his reindeer as quickly as possible, but everyone else can hinder him by getting in his way.

The Christmas Tree Is Home Base

Rules of the Game:

One person tries to catch the others. Anyone who manages to touch a Christmas tree cannot be caught. 3-5 people wearing twigs and/or tinsel in their hair represent the Christmas trees – home bases.

Decorative Christmas Balls Are Home Base

Rules of the Game:

One person – the catcher – tries to catch the others. Anyone holding a softball (= a decorative Christmas ball decoration) in their hands cannot be caught. The softball must be thrown to anyone who is threatened with being caught.

Variations:
- 1-3 catchers
- 1-3 softballs

Father Christmas Looks for Helpers

Rules of the Game:

4-8 teams are formed to play a 'chain' relay race. The first person in each group is Father Christmas, identifiable by wearing a Father Christmas hood and/or a cotton wool beard. He runs round a turning point and back again to fetch a 'helper'.

Now they run together as a pair round the turning point and back to fetch another helper and so on and so forth until the last person has been collected. The team that wins is the first to get back to the start with the whole group still holding hands.

The Advent Relay Race

Rules of the Game:

Carry out a relay race using a burning candle as a baton. The burning candle has to be handed over to the next player in the team as fast as possible.

Variations:
- Run normally.
- Run backwards.
- Slalom.
- Drive on pedal-vehicles.
- Race on trolleys etc.

A Sledging Relay Race

Rules of the Game:
One person sits on a skateboard or a flat trolley. The partner pulls the skateboard round the hall by a rope.

Variations:
- Go round a turning point.
- Do it as a slalom.
- Do it as Father Christmas's sleigh with presents on; e.g., presents = rice sacks to be brought back.

The Christmas Treat Relay

Rules of the Game:
At the turning point in the relay race a Christmas treat has to be eaten (mince pies, shortbread, cinnamon biscuits etc).

Variations:
- A running relay race.
- As a slalom.
- Use pedal-vehicles to go on.
- Pulled along using a skateboard (see 'Sledging Relay Race') etc.

Carrying Christmas Decorations

Rules of the Game:
Using a balloon to represent a Christmas decoration, these have to be carried round a turning point.

Variations:
- The balloon can be carried in different ways: balanced on the palm of the hand, moving along striking the balloon in the air to keep it moving with you, using the head to move the balloon.
- Slalom.
- Driving on a pedal-vehicle ...

Singing Christmas Songs under Water

Rules of the Game:
Since many of these Christmas games can be played also under water, here is one that can only be played under water and simply because of this has a particular appeal. Everyone is standing in a circle in the paddling pool. At a signal they all duck under the water. One of them 'sings' a Christmas song under water and the others have to guess which one it is.

Are You Father Christmas?

Rules of the Game:
The exercise leader explains "You all know that Father Christmas is a generous man and can often work wonders. Now we are all going to play being blind and run round the room with closed eyes. When we bump into a Father Christmas and touch him we are able to see again and turn into a Father Christmas. When we bump into someone we must immediately ask, "Are you Father Christmas?" If that person answers "No!", then we have to carry on looking for someone, who when asked for a second time does not answer with "No!" – because this will be Father Christmas.

Father Christmas – the Rescuer

Rules of the Game:
The catcher is the Christmas postman who tries to catch everyone and give him or her a 'Christmas card'. Everyone he touches stands still and holds up their hands. Amongst the players is someone, who unbeknown to the catcher was chosen as Father Christmas beforehand, and he can free them. The game is ended when the postman finds Father Christmas.

Variations:
- Two postmen.
- Two Father Christmas's.
- Anyone having a beard is Father Christmas.

Find Father Christmas

Rules of the Game:
All move round the room with closed eyes and try to find Father Christmas. Father Christmas (who could be e.g., the exercise supervisor) has 'hidden' himself earlier in the darkened room – he simply sits down anywhere in the room. Whoever finds Father Christmas sits down next to him and can 'see' again.

The series of Christmas and winter theme games can finish up by holding a good coffee party and trying out the Christmas goodies (mince pies, shortbread etc).

3. The Carnival

Family sports sessions that take place around the time of a carnival (Mardi Gras, Harvest festival etc.) can take on the time of year as a theme. Everyone can dress up accordingly. Some games come to life by virtue of the costumes being worn by the participants. Here are a few examples:

Building Groups

Rules of the Game:
All move round in the room to the rhythm of the music. When the music stops the following groups have to be built up according to fancy dress.
• All the red Indians.
• All the cowboys.
• All the clowns etc .

The groups now have to carry out various movement tasks:
• Move together as a group.
• Circle round another group.
• Using the members of the group, form a carnival float .

Catch the Jester

Rules of the Game:
Someone plays the court "Jester" and starts to catch the others. Anyone caught holds hands with the "Jester" and catches with him (same as 'Chain Catch' – see Data Bank).

Who's Afraid of Ash Wednesday?

Rules of the Game:
All the "Carnival revellers" stand on one side of the hall, and someone representing 'Ash Wednesday' – the catcher – stands on the other. The catcher calls out "Who's afraid of Ash Wednesday?" Everyone answers "No one". He answers "What happens when it comes?" Everyone answers "We run away". Anyone caught by the catcher turns into a catcher as an Ash Wednesday man.

Mardi Gras, Oh Mardi Gras – Which Flag Is Flying Today?

Rules of the Game:
The catcher stands on one side of the hall with all the others on the opposite side. Everyone calls out to the catcher "Mardi Gras, Oh Mardi Gras – Which Flag Is Flying Today?" The catcher calls out a colour. Anyone wearing something with that colour

can be caught as he runs over to the other side. Those caught now help the catcher. (Change the theme to "Fisherman, Fisherman – What Flag Are You Showing Today?").

Cowboys and Red Indians

Rules of the Game:
Two groups stand along the middle line of the gymnasium hall about 1-2 m from each other. According to the fancy dress, one group are red Indians and the other cowboys. (The game is the same as "Black and White" or "Winter – Christmas" – see Data Bank).

The Sweetie Relay

Rules of the Game:
Carry out a relay race so that at the turning point sweeties, chocolates or other carnival bonbons have to be collected.

Variations:
• Run normally.
• Run backwards.
• Run along on all fours .
• Use pedal-vehicles.
• Link arms with someone else.

Further Games:
• Up I Stretch .
• Gin-gan Gooli.
• Stepping over Stepping Stones.

To round off a carnival day it is a good idea to hold an outdoors sunny coffee party.

4.   Further Projects

• Sports Studio

Groups can be formed to collect ideas and contributions and work up themes to put into the "Sports Studio". Workshops like these can work on the following ideas as themes:

*   Reporting a downhill skiing event
*   Sports acrobatics
*   A horse show
*   The 100 metres running race – in slow motion
*   Prize giving
*   National dancing
*   The weather forecast – and any other ideas which involve sports and games.

Ideas for these themes are put together and rehearsed in the workshop. They are then put together in a programme for the 'Sports Studio'. The presenter leads during the programme and announces each of the contributions as they come forward. If a programme of this kind is recorded on video, a 'live' atmosphere can be created.

• The Jungle

Form groups who work on 'jungle' themes in a workshop. These are then acted out in activities and games. The following suggestions can be used to form groups.

*   Dance of the jungle apes
*   Elephants
*   Swinging through the jungle on liana (like Tarzan)
*   In the deepest jungle
*   On the banks of the torrent
*   Tigers and other wild animals
*   Jungle natives
*   Crocodiles.

The group's ideas can be assembled into 'stands' around the jungle. The whole group now moves round from jungle 'stand' to jungle 'stand' where each of the themes is enacted.

• The Wild West

Form groups, as workshops, to work on ideas for the theme "The Wild West". The following are suggested ideas for this theme:

- Using the lasso and breaking-in wild mustangs
- Red Indians
- Duels
- On the prairie
- Building the railways
- Stalking
- Buffalo hunting.

The group's ideas can be put together into a programme of "Wild West" situations. The whole group moves round from event to event where each of the themes is enacted.

• Further Games:

Pirates on an island, the cruise ship, 'Adventure Island', Himalayan expedition etc.

IV.   Integrated Family Sport

Part 4:   Activities outside the Gymnasium

There is a multitude of activities that the family sports group can take part in besides the regular sports afternoons in the gymnasium. In the Paderborn Family Sports Group, a mother's meeting has been built up from the contacts they have made during the sporting activities with each other. This meets regularly once a month.

At these meetings they can have a 'natter', exchange experiences and discuss common problems and obtain tips about various things e.g., schooling, local administrative matters etc. Within this group, a flautist group has been formed who play together and have taken part playing at church services and other events where they can show off their talents.

In the following sections there is a description of the four particular aspects that the Paderborn model use to complement and enrich the activities of the family sports group. Most of the activities, moreover, are very suitable to intensify contacts amongst the members, to make it easier to integrate new members and also to work up ideas and proposals.

• Family leisure time
• Swimming
• Walking
• Fun-fairs / giant bouncy airbeds

1.   Family Leisure Time

One or twice a year the family sports group organises a so-called 'Family Leisure Time'. This can be over a weekend or a week long. These events can best be held in sports stadiums or places/buildings where there are opportunities to carry out sports. In Germany the facilities offered by the Youth Centre at Hardehausen, or the Leisure Centre of the Disabled Sports Club at Schieder-Schwalenberg on the Emmerstausee, are good examples.

Some facilities offer meals and in others this has to be arranged by the organisers. In some ways this requirement can provide an added incentive for integration.

Picture 17: Family leisure time at the Emmerstausee

In addition to the early reservation of such a facility, the selection of a good organising team is very important for the success of the leisure period. In the organising team there should be the sports teachers, training assistants, one or two parent representatives and some child-minders. The latter are able to keep the disabled and the able bodied children occupied for a while whenever the parents gather together for discussion groups or other activities. According to the size of the group the organising team should be about 4-8 strong.

Prior to the actual leisure period there should be a meeting of all those who will be taking part in the leisure time. At this meeting the aims and expectations of the period should be explained, and everyone will have the opportunity to make their own suggestions. In this way a draft programme can be put together that, of course, can be adjusted at any time according to requirements and the situation on the actual day.

The periods can be run along particular themes or to emphasise certain things. The Paderborn group up until now has mainly used the following themes:
- Structure of leisure activities
- Integration into everyday life
- Lifestyle of the disabled
- The disabled and sexuality
- In addition there has been a multitude of leisure activities that have been exclusively organised for recreation and rest purposes.

By looking at an example of the daily programme of a family leisure period one gains a good insight into the sequence of events:

Diagram 9: Daily Programme

7.30	Early morning gymnastics/a run in the woods (voluntary)
8.00	Reveille (with music)
9.00	Morning song and breakfast
10.00	Joint walk or discussion group for the parents/handicrafts for the children (run in parallel)
12.30	Lunch followed by a rest
15.00	Coffee break
15.30	Joint sports activities; e.g., swimming or silk-screen painting for the grown-ups/painting and games for the children
18.00	Evening meal
19.00	Joint evening with singing, games and dancing
20.30	Games, singing and parents' 'natter'

In addition to such or similar programmes the actual location can offer other special activities e.g., in Germany at Schieder one can take a cruise boat or journey by train from Schieder to Hameln to see the Rat-catcher's House.

Leisure periods of this type are the 'icing on the cake' for family sports groups. They offer an opportunity for the group to thoroughly enjoy communication, social togetherness, companionship, openness and fun. Moreover the contacts already built up between individual families can be strengthened and developed. This lends normal family sport a positive atmosphere.

2.   Swimming

The visit to a public swimming pool offers a good opportunity for integrated family sports groups to venture into the public and take part in something together with other able bodied people. Spontaneous contact by the disabled children and youths comes automatically and normally with the other swimming pool visitors. These can be inspired to join in the games. The young bathing pool visitors particularly show an interest in joining in the games spontaneously, and thus learn, casually, to get on with disabled children and youths. They learn to accept them as equal human beings. We have experienced that on such occasions when the games in which others spontaneously took part were over, everyone was sorry to see them finish.

The following games are those suitable as integrated games at the swimming pool. They are played in the paddling pool so that everyone can take part – even water-shy children or grown-ups and non-swimmers.

Eeny Miny Mo
Rules of the Game:
All the players hold hands in a circle. One player starts off in the middle as the catcher. Everyone now sings and hops to the words:

> *"Eeny miny mo*
> *A fish has bit my toe*
> *eeny miny mick*
> *Swim away quick."*

At the last word everyone tries to reach the edge of the pool running or swimming as quickly as possible, while the catcher tries to catch at least one before he does so. If he is successful the person caught becomes the new catcher.

Variations:
• Sing loudly and jump up and down.
• Sing softly and just jump up and down a little.
• All people caught stay as catchers so that the number of catchers gradually increases.

The second verse of the song is:

> *"Eeny miny mail*
> *The fish shakes its tail (everyone splashes the catcher in the middle)*
> *eeny miny mick*
> *Swim away quick."*

Show Your Feet
Rules of the Game:
All stand in a circle and sing the songs below. The players do actions to represent the songs which help those learning to get used to being in water.

> *"Show your feet (everyone lifts the right foot)*
> *Show your shoes (everyone lifts the left foot)*
> *And let's see what we can do:*

(1) I'm going to wash that man right out of my hair ... (All do the actions of washing the hair, face and other parts of the body)

(2) Dashing away with the smoothing iron ... (All do the actions of ironing close over the surface of the water and thus create splashing everywhere)

(3) I'm forever blowing bubbles ... (All blow air into the water to make bubbles)

(4) I could have danced all night ... (All dance around in twos or threes holding on to each other)

(5) And so on and so forth ...

"What's the Time Mr. Shark?"

Rules of the Game:
One child is the shark and places him/herself at one end of the pool facing away from the others. The other children stand in the water on the opposite side of the pool. The children call out to the shark, "What's the time Mr. Shark?" He calls out a time that he chooses. The children wade forward before the shark turns around but stop once he faces them. The shark will choose when to call "dinner time" at which all children have to try to get back to their side of the pool before being caught.

The Sea Calls all Fish

Rules of the Game:
Each child can choose which sort of fish he/she wishes to be. The dolphins, the plaice, the goldfish or the sole and each chooses a corner of the swimming pool. The leader stays in the middle and is the 'Sea'. The 'Sea' calls all the fish into the water. The fish copy all actions performed by the 'Sea'. For example, the sea is calm to begin with and all the fish are lying still on the surface of the water.

The sea starts to make small waves. The wind begins to blow and the waves become bigger, a storm is brewing and the waves become even bigger. This can develop into a hurricane. When the 'Sea' calls out "high tide!" all the fish have to swim back to their corner before being stranded and caught. Those that are caught help the 'Sea' to catch the remaining fish.

"Fisherman, Fisherman – How Deep Is the Water?"

Rules of the Game:
The fisherman – the catcher – stands on one side of the paddling pool with all the others on the opposite side. All shout out "Fisherman, Fisherman – how deep is the water?" The fisherman answers e.g., "A thousand fathoms". They all then ask, "How do I get across?" The fisherman then gives an answer which indicates the way they have to come across – e.g., "Hop on one leg"; "Backwards"; "Make paddling motions with your arms" or "Underwater" etc. Those caught have to help the catcher.

Duck Shooting

Rules of the Game:
The hunter tries to catch the others who are ducks. When the hunter comes by they can duck i.e., whoever has his head under the water cannot be caught.

Variation: • The hunter 'shoots' with a soft water ball.

Further Running and Catching Games:
   • Chain Catch
   • Catching and Freeing
   • Magic Mouse
   • Chain Catch in Pairs
   • Black and White
   • ABC
   • "Help me!"
   • Ball Possession – Taboo
   • Catching and Freeing Using a Home Base
   • See also Games – Data Bank

Flying Fish

Rules of the Game:
All the players form a narrow lane. Each person joins hands across the gap. Another person lies on the outstretched arms which throw him up and forward down the lane like flying fish.

Chain Relay

Rules of the Game:
Several relay teams are formed – each at least five persons strong. The first person runs or swims to the other side of the pool and back. The second person holds on to the first and they go to the other side and back again together. Then a third person holds on and joins in and so on .... Which team gets through first with all its members still holding on together?

Carrying Relay

Rules of the Game:
Various objects have to be carried along in this relay race: swimming floats, swimming aids, paddles, lilos, diving masks, balls etc.

Variations:
- A number of objects are added; the first person uses the swimming float and hands it over to the second person who must carry a ball as well. The third person adds another object and so on.
- Burning night lights have to be transported on the swimming float.

Dressing up Relay: each relay swimmer has to put on a T-shirt, flippers and don a hat before he swims off. These have to be taken off and handed over to the second man who puts them on – and so on.

Water Biathlon

Rules of the Game:
This biathlon relay race takes place in the water. The relay swimmers swim a certain distance and then have to throw 1-3 times at a target e.g., a basketball basket. Every time he misses he has to do an extra length.

Variations:
- Various types of target; water basketball target, large hoops, washing baskets, swimming floats or swimming aids placed on the side of the pool.
- Swimming the length without a ball using a particular stroke or dribbling the ball.

Further Relay Races: See Data Bank.

3. Hiking

A further possibility for the expansion of the family sports programme is outdoor hiking together. The Paderborn Family Sports Group organises a hike at least once a year in a lovely part of the region around Paderborn. The start and finish is often at a sports field so that one has the opportunity, before and after, to play together or let the children play, as well as to just have discussions or catch up with contacts.

Very often a hiking outing like this will end up by holding a barbecue to make sure that the social side of life is not excluded.

An interesting variant of the hike is the "ABC Hike". Before the hike, groups are formed who go off together and have the task of finding something on the hike to bring back which represents each of the letters in the alphabet, and which they have to enter in a list.

Tiger Ball

Rules of the Game:
The members of a team stand in a circle and throw the ball to each other. Another person stands in the middle of the circle and tries to deflect the ball or catch it. If he manages to touch or catch the ball then the person who threw the ball goes into the middle as the new tiger.

Variations:
* Only throwing at reachable heights is allowed.
* The number of 'tigers' is increased to 2-4.
* People in the circle throw and catch in the sitting position.
* The game is played in two circles. The 'tiger' comes from the opposing team each time – with changeovers from the home team each time a ball is caught. The winning team is the one that has had the most tigers in the opposing team's circle.
* Everyone plays the game in wheelchairs.

Ball on the Castle

Rules of the Game:
A medicine ball is placed on top of a box or a built-up mound. Around this, 5-12 players stand and try to knock the ball off by throwing balls at it. A defender tries to prevent them doing so by deflecting the balls.

Variations:
* Only balls caught cleanly by the players may be used to throw at the medicine ball.
* Two or three defenders.
* All the players are in wheelchairs.

Tower Ball

Rules of the Game:
Two teams play against each other. Each team tries to throw the ball to his own goalkeeper who is standing on a box. Every time the goalkeeper catches the ball the team scores a point.

Variations:
* Before the team can take a shot for their own goalkeeper to catch the ball, they must have passed the ball within their own team at least 6-10 times .
* Before each team member can throw the ball to the goalkeeper he must have had contact with the ball at least once previously.

- The goalkeeper has to sit on the box.
- When playing the game in water the goalkeeper sits on the poolside.
- When playing the game in wheelchairs, the goalkeeper is on a mat or in some other marked out area.

The Moving Basket
Rules of the Game:
A basket (waste paper basket, upturned cone) is fixed to the back of each of the children's wheelchairs. An equal number of rice sacks or similar objects is shared out to the two teams. The aim is to get as many rice sacks as possible into the 'baskets' of the opposing team. Everybody can move freely round the hall taking care not to have a rice sack being placed in his or her basket. Teams can defend their own baskets. If a rice sack falls on the ground anybody can pick it up and claim it. When all the sacks are in the baskets they are counted up.

Variation: • Tie baskets to the backs of people.

Biathlon
Rules of the Game:
Form 2-6 teams of 3-10 players each. They run a relay race where the first person carries or dribbles a ball over a certain distance. At the end he has three shots at knocking over, for example, cones on a bench. Each time he misses he has to complete a penalty distance.

Variations:
- Various targets: hoops, basketball nets, traffic cones, small goal posts ...
- Vary the distance to run: in length, as a slalom, as an obstacle course.
- Carry the ball in front of or behind the body, on or over the head, between the legs.
- Dribble the ball.
- Play the game in wheelchairs.

Further Small Ball Games:
"Tired, Worn out, Dead"; Group Ball Game; Fireball; Völker Ball (see Data Bank).
• **Games with Additional Equipment.**

Games with the parachute are very popular for integrated wheelchair players (see chapter B.I.4.2).

Strengthening the Chest Muscles
Holding the palm of the one hand upwards at chin height, place the palm of the other hand on top of it and press slowly downwards as far as hip height, resisting by pressing the lower hand upwards as much as possible. Repeat using opposite hands.

Stretching the Back Muscles
Grasp the hands behind the back of the head and press the head between the legs. Hold for ten seconds.

Strengthening the Support Muscles of the Arms, Chest and Back
The hands grasp the propelling rings of the wheelchair and push yourself up out of the chair. "Who can hold the position for the longest?"

Variation:
• Place your weight over the right hand and then over the left hand.

Loosening the Arms and Shoulders
Do various stretching exercises with the arms: flex the arm forwards, backwards, alternately, slowly, quickly.

Loosening the Shoulder Joints
• Circle the arms forward, backwards (both arms together).
• Windmill the arms forwards, backwards.
• Pedal the arms: one circles forwards and the other backwards.

Strengthening the Grip
Grip with outstretched arms: to the front, to the rear, upward, to the side.

5.   Games

Shuttlecock/Badminton
Play games with badminton racquets and balloons.

Wheelchair Basketball
Team training has already been experienced and exercised in the games 'Tiger Ball' and 'Simple Group Ball Games'. We saw the introduction of an opposing team in the 'Tiger Ball' game. If the number of opponents increases until both teams are the same size we find we are ready for the 'Simple Group Ball Game'. If we move onto 'Fire-Ball' we eventually recognise that we can use the basketball backboard. If we move slowly through the rules of basketball we can build up to a proper game of wheelchair basketball. Since the rules for wheelchair basketball are almost identical to the "pedestrian's" version, this means that they can easily play wheelchair basketball without any problem.

Further Games
Table tennis, from 'Ball over the Rope' to volleyball, from rolling the ball at a goal to handball (see the Data Bank: Ball Games).

6.   Activities outside the Gymnasium

Family Leisure Periods
In the same way as sport for the family, family leisure periods are an important element of joint activities for the integration of children's wheelchair groups, and this increases the social cohesion of the group.

Wheelchair Orienteering ━━━━━━━━━━━━━━━━━━━━━━━━━━━━━
In our integrated wheelchair group we also try out new types of sport that can provide a stimulus for the togetherness of disabled and able bodied people.

Together with the German National Trainer for Orienteering we have carried out several orienteering events using the wheelchair. Here are two possibilities for such a wheelchair orienteering event.

• Point Orienteering
Point orienteering is carried out by driving around a course without setting a time restriction. The course can be marked out using directional arrows on the side of the

C.   Organisation of an Integrated Sports Group

This chapter aims to give some practical tips about how to bring an integrated sports group to life and how to organise it. It also aims to answer the question about what aspects have to be present in the way of organisational factors when getting down to the business of beginning to practice sport e.g., family sport.

The question whether to form a unique club or join an existing sports club, and what assistance one can expect from authorities, particularly for the integrated groups and sports groups for the disabled, will be covered at the end.

First of all the demand for sport to be provided in an integrated group and for families must be assessed. In Germany there are very few family sports groups at all, and even fewer who offer sport for the disabled.

If sports groups for children and youths are to be formed as a result of initiatives by interested persons, such as parents, family members or establishments involved in the care of the disabled, several important points should be noted. It will be soon established that the founding of groups of this type will be difficult. The difficulties will stem from not only a general reservation and a lack of preparedness by some sports clubs to accept these groups, but also the ability to procure suitable facilities and equipment. Collaboration with sports clubs, specific public relations work, a great deal of commitment, and above all, a gift of the powers of persuasion for the requirement of such an arrangement, will all be critical and decisive from the beginning, if the project is to come to fruition. Using the example of family sports, the following shows how sport can be built up into an integrated group.

1. Formation

First of all, a circle of parents and families has to be found who are interested in leisure and family sport. This can happen in a number of ways:

- Several families, who already know each other, can join together with a sports instructor and plan the family sports event, and open this up to other families.
- A teacher, sports instructor or the local headmaster may offer to organise a leisure and sports weekend for families of one of their classes. During this the essential elements of family sport can be experienced, and perhaps this will whet their appetites for the requirement to be a regular occurrence for the whole family.

- A further possibility for the initiation of a family sports group is to organise a leisure week or weekend. This can be carried out with the help of parents of children in a class together with the teachers, and eventually the assistance of experts in the field such as social or youth workers.

If as a result of getting to know each other better during the period and the necessary interest has developed, this can be turned into a regular affair with a family sports group being the end product.

2. Prerequisites

If family sport is to become a regular occurrence, a gymnasium will be required. At the beginning a small hall or part of a larger gymnasium will suffice. This is the way that the "Paderborn Family Sports Group" started out, managing by using the small gymnasium of a School for Special Needs before obtaining the use of the large gymnasium, with its three sections, at the University Polytechnic of Paderborn.

It is advisable to reserve a slot in the programme of a facility with its administrators as early on as possible. It is probably a common problem to break into the bookings in such establishments with a new group. Possibly you will be able eventually to secure slots to run "Sunday morning action periods" to start off the group before being able to obtain a regular slot in the gymnasium programme. Using the smaller 'starter' group, this can gradually be expanded.

3. Leadership

It is usually normal, certainly in Germany where it is a matter of law, that the sports group has to be supervised by a trained and qualified instructor. If the group includes activities for the disabled, then the instructor must possess the applicable additional qualifications demanded by the relevant authorities.

In addition to a suitably qualified instructor the group will require assistants and helpers. It is advisable to check whether there are legal requirements, which could be either a national or simply a local prerequisite, for these important assistants, especially if they are to have a hand in the practical side of conducting exercises, particularly for children. The availability of assistants is always a good way of taking the pressure off parents, if at least it is only for a short time – a valuable breathing space where the disabled are involved. The number of assistants and helpers required

5. Finances

The existence of a family sports group for disabled people is not only dependent on the factors already mentioned such as an instructor, a gymnasium and an organisational structure, it largely is a question of finance. Besides paying for instructor's fees, rent of the facility, subscriptions to national organisations and other similar expenditure, there is the requirement to hold a contingency fund for unplanned or special events and matters such as leisure periods, laying in a stock of club T-shirts and track suits. Above all the most important pillar of financial support will be the member's contributions. Normally the club can decide what these are to be. In Germany, where subsidies from national organisations are forthcoming, then membership fees have to be maintained at certain levels to qualify for that sponsorship. The reader of this book, if not already in possession of such material, must ensure that he/she has thoroughly researched the subject of founding a family sports group. He/she must ensure that, in the end, all taking part are properly protected, not only from the financial and legal aspect, but also from disappointment in the expectations they set out to achieve.

Credits – Tables, Diagrams and Pictures

Pictures 8 & 18	– Dirk van Ophuysen
Pictures 5,6,7,9-13	– Jan-Bernd Uptmoor
Pictures 14 & 15	– Bernd Braune
Pictures 1-4,16,17,19	– Uwe Rheker
Diagrams 2 -7	– Rebecca Rheker
Diagrams 1,8 -10	– Achim Beule
Tables 2-4	– Achim Beule

D.   GAMES – DATA BANK

2. Games in Water

3. Games with a Partner

4. Games for Small Groups

5. Team Games

9. Games to Music

10. Games with Psychomotor Exercise Equipment

11. Running and Chasing Games

12. Catching and Throwing Games

13. Acting Games

14. Dancing and Singing Games

15. Games to Improve Communication

16. Interactive Games

17. Competitive Games

Name of the game   *Page*

18. Projects and Games
Name of the game **Page**

19. Games to Experience the Physique
Name of the game **Page**

20. Games to Experience Equipment

21. Games for Social Experience

22 Games suitable for the Wheelchair

23. Ball Games in the Water

24. Gymnasium Games with Psychomotor Equipment

LANGE, J.: Schwimmen - Teil des Handlungsfeldes Sport. In: VOLCK, G. (Hrsg.): Schwimmen in der Schule. Schorndorf 1977, 9-40.

LÖWISCH, D.-J.: Pädagogisches Heilen. München 1969.

MAIKOWSKI, R./PODLESCH, W.: Geistig behinderte Kinder in der Grundschule?. In: EBERWEIN, H. (Hrsg.): Behinderte und Nichtbehinderte lernen gemeinsam. Handbuch der Interationspädagogik. Weinheim /Basel 1990 (2. Aufl.), 261-267.

MERTENS, K.: Körperwahrnehmung und Körpergeschick, Dortmund 1991 (2.Aufl.).

MICHELS, F.: Ergebnisse der Befragung zur Freizeit- und Bildungsarbeit mit geistigbehinderten Erwachsenen in Paderborn, (nichveröffentlichter Bericht einer Projektgruppe der KFH Paderborn) 1988.

NIEDERBRACHT, H.: Segeln mit Behinderten und Nichtbehinderten. Lüneburg 1987.

NIRJE, B./PERRIN, B.: Das Normalisierungsprinzip und seine Mißverständnisse. In: ZUSAMMEN 6 (1986) 7, 8-9

NIRJE, B.: Das Normalisierungsprinzip und seine Auswirkungen in der fürsorglichen Betreuung. In: KUGEL, R. B./WOLFENSBERGER, W.(Hrsg.): Geistig Behinderte – Eingliederung oder Bewahrung. Stuttgart 1974, 23-26.

OFFERMANN, D.: Zur Thorie und Praxis einer „Integrativen Behindertenpädagogik". In: KASZTANTOWICZ, U. (Hrsg.): Wege aus der Isolation, Konzepte und Analysen der Integration Behinderter in Dänemark. Heidelberg 1986, 27-55.

OPASCHOWSKI, H. W.: Pädagogik der Freizeit. Bad Heilbrunn 1976.

OPASCHOWSKI, H. W.: Pädagogik und Didaktik der Freizeit. Opladen 1987.

RECKENWALD, H. C.: Ökonomische   Wissenschaft und technisch-politische Evolution. Düsseldorf 1989.

RHEKER, U.: Freizeitspiele - Möglichkeiten zur Integration behinderter Kinder und Jugendlicher. In: SPORTPÄDAGOGIK 1/1980.

RHEKER, U.: Familiensportgruppe mit behinderten und nichtbehinderten Kindern. In: BÖS, K. u.a.: Geistig Behinderte in Bewegung, Spiel und Sport. Duisburg 1989 (a), 123-146.

RHEKER, U.: Bewegung, Spiel und Sport mit behinderten Kindern und Jugendlichen. In: MOTORIK. 12 (1989) 1 (b), 19-24

RHEKER, U.: Integrativer Familiensport – Bewegung, Spiel und Sport für Familien mit behinderten und nichtbehinderten Kindern. In: DIE SPORTSTUNDE – Anregungen für die Sportpraxis, 101 Beilage zur Zeitschrift: BEHINDERUNG UND SPORT 7/8 (1991) (a), 1-8.

RHEKER, U.: Rollstuhl-Orientungslauf – eine neue Rollstuhlsportart. In: BEHINDERUNG UND SPORT 10 (1991) (b), 202-203.

RHEKER, U.: Modelle als Normalität – integrativer Behindertensport in Paderborn. In: DOLL-TEPPER/LIENERT, CH.: Sport von Menschem mit geistiger Behinderung – Situationen und Trends. Marburg 1991 (c), 79-87.

RUNDE, P./HEINZE, R. G. (Hrsg.): Chancengleichheit für Behinderte, Sozialwissenschaftliche Analyse für die Praxis. Neuwied/Darmstadt 1979.

RUSCH, H./GRÖSSING, S.: Sport mit Körperbehinderten. Schorndorf 1991.

RUSCH, H./SPERLE, N. (Red.): Behindertensport an Hochschulen. Ahrensburg 1988.

SANDER, A.: Behinderungsbegriffe und ihre Konsequenzen für die Integration. In: EBERWEIN, H. (Hrsg.): Behinderte und Nichtbehinderte lernen gemeinsam. Handbuch der Integrationspädagogik, Weinheim/Basel 1990 (2. Aufl.), 75-82.

SCHICK, E.-M.: Zur Bewegungserziehung in der Familie. Schorndorf 1981.

SCHMEICHEL, M.: Regelschule oder Sonderschule – zur pädagogischen Förderung körperbehinderter Kinder. In: DAS BAND 3 (1983), 16-22.

SCHÖLER, J.: Nichtaussonderung von Kindern und Jugendlichen mit besonderen pädagogischen Bedürfnissen. In: EBERWEIN, H. (Hrsg.): Behinderte und Nichtbehinderte lernen gemeinsam. Handbuch der Integrationspäkagogik, Weinheim/Basel 1990 (2. Aufl.), 83-90.

GRUPE, O./GABLER, H. GÖHNER, U. (Hrsg.): Spiel-Spiele-Spielen. Schorndorf 1983.

GUTIERREZ, G.: Theologie der Befreiung, München 1982 (6. Aufl.)

HAEP, H.: Gegen scheinbare Integration zur Imageverbesserung. In: BEHINDERUNG UND SPORT 8 (1987), 181.

HAEP, H.: Neue Richtlinien. In: BEHINDERUNG UND SPORT 1(1991), 5 (a).

HAEP, H.: Hinweise zur Anwendung znd Auslegung der Gesamtvereinbarung über den ambulanten Behindertensport. In: „BEHINDERUNG UND SPORT" 7/8 (1991), (b), 138-139.

HECKER, G. u.a.: Schulsport-Leistungssport-Breitensport. St. Augustin 1983.

HOF, B.: Kritische Entgegnung. In: RECKENWALD, H. C.: Ökonomische Wissenschaft und technisch-politische Evolution. Düsseldorf 1989, 161-175.

INSTITUT DER DEUTSCHEN WIRTSCHAFT KÖLN: Zahlen zur wirtschaftlichen Entwicklung der Bundesrepublik Deutschland 1990.

INTERESSENGEMEINSCHAFT BEHINDERTER STUDENTEN BERLIN (Hrsg.): Erfahrungsaustausch behinderter Studenten in Ost und West Tagung 90. Berlin 1990

IRMISCHER, T.: Motopädagogik bei geistig Behinderten. Schorndorf 1980.

IRMISCHER, T.: Bewegungserziehung an der Schule für Geistigbehinderte. Dortmund 1981.

IRMISCHER, T./FISCHER, K.: Psychomotorik in der Entwicklung. Schorndorf 1989.

JACOBI, P./RÖSCH, H.-E.: Sport und Menschenwürde. Mainz 1982.

JACOBSON: Progressive relaxation. Chicago 1948.

JANSEN, G. W.: Die Einstellung der Gesellschaft zu Körperbehinderten. Eine psychologische Analyse zwischenmenschlicher Beziehungen aufgrund emprischer Untersuchungen, Rheinstetten 1981 (4. Aufl.)

KAPUSTIN, P.: Familie und Sport. Aachen 1991.

KARL, H.: Die schulische und außerschulische Situation körperbehinderter Kinder und Jugendlicher unter Berücksichtigung entwicklungs- und sozialpsychologischer Aspekte. In: RUSCH, H. /GRÖSSING, S.: Sport mit Körperbehinderten. Schorndorf 1991, 15-40.

KASZTANTOWICZ, U. (Hrsg.): Wege aus der Isolation, Konzepte und Analysen der Integration Behinderter in Dänemark. Heidelberg 1986.

KERKHOFF, W. (Hrsg.): Freizeitchancen und Freizeitlernen für behinderte Kinder und Jugendliche. Berlin 1982.

KIPHARD, E.J.: Motopädagogik. Dortmund 1979.

KIPHARD, E.J.: Mototherapie, Bd. I und II. Dortmund 1983.

KIPHARD, E.J.: Psychomotorik in Praxis und Theorie. Gütersloh, 1989.

KLEE, E.: Behindert. Über die Enteignung von Körper und Bewußtsein. Frankfurt a. M. 1980.

KLEE, E.: Behinderten-Report. Frankfurt 1989.

KOSEL, E.: Behindertensport. München 1981.

KUGEL, R. B./WOLFENBERGER, W. (Hrsg.): Geistig Behinderte – Eingliederung oder Bewahrung. Stuttgart 1974.

KURZ, D./ VOLCK, G.: Zur didaktischen Begründung des Schwimmens in der Schule. In: VOLCK, G. (Hrsg.): Schwimmen in der Schule. Schorndorf 1977, 41-58.

KURZ, D.: Elemente des Schulsports. Schorndorf 1979 (2. Aufl.)

E. Literature

1. Theory

ASCHER, G: Medizinische Aspekte beim Sport mit körperbehinderten Kindern und Jugendlichen. In: RUSCH, H./GRÖSSING, S.: Sport mit Körperbehinderten. Schorndorf 1991, 41-54.

BÄCHTHOLD, A./MATTMÜLLER, F.: Alle reden über Integration ... Berlin 1984.

BELLEBAUM, A: Soziologische Grundbegriffe. Stuttgart/Berlin/Köln/Mainz 1974.

BERNSTEIN, D.A./BORKOVEC, TH. D: Entspannungs-Training. München 1978.

BLEIDICK, U.: Theorie der Behindertenpädagogik. 1985.

BLEIDICK, U. (Hrsg.): Eine Standortbestimmung der Behindertenpädagogik, U. Bleidich über O. Specks Buch "System Heilpädagogik". In: ZUSAMMEN 5 (1989), 25-26.

BÖS, K. u.a.: Geistig Behinderte in Bewegung, Spiel und Sport. Duisburg 1989.

BRETTSCHNEIDER, W.-.D./BRÄUTIGAM, M.: Sport im Alltag von Jugendlichen. Schorndorf 1989 (a).

BRETTSCHNEIDER, W.-.D./BAUR, J./ BRÄUTIGAM, M. (Red.): Bewegungswelt von Kindern und Jugendlichen. Schorndorf 1989 (b).

BRETTSCHNEIDER, W.-D./BRÄUTIGAM, M.: Sport in der Alltagswelt von Jugendlichen, Schriftenreihe vom Kultusministerium NRW. H. 27, Frechen 1990.

BUNDESMINISTER FÜR ARBEIT UND SOZIALORDNUNG (Hrsg.): Weltaktionsprogramm für Behinderte, Jahrzehnt der Behinderten der Vereinten Nationen 1983-1990. Bonn 1983.

CLOERKES, G.: Einstellung und Verhalten gegenüber Körperbehinderten. Eine Bestandsaufnahme der Ergebnisse internatioler Forschung. 3. Aufl. Berlin 1985.

CLOERKES, G.: Sozio-kulturelle Bedingungen für die Entstehung von Einstellungen gegenüber Behinderten. In: VIERTELJAHRESZEITSCHRIFTEN FÜR HEILPÄDAGOGIK, 49 (1980) 3, 259-273.

CLOERKES, G.: Einstellungen gegenüber Behinderten und mögliche Strategien zu ihrer Veränderung. In: MEDIZIN, MENSCH, GESELLSCHAFT 8(1983), 271-279.

COMEBACK: Sport für Behinderte. München 1988.

DEUTSCHER BILDUNGSRAT (Hrsg.): Empfehlungen der Bildungskommission „Zur pädagogischen Förderung behinderter und von Behinderung bedrohter Kinder und Jugendlicher". Bonn 1990.

DOLL-TEPPER G./LIENERT, CH.: Sport von Menschen mit geistiger Behinderung – Situationen und Trends. Marburg 1991.

DREYER, A. u.a.: Warum nicht so? Geistigbehinderte in Dänemark. Solms-Oberbiel 1981.

EBERWEIN, H. (Hrsg.): Behinderte und Nichtbehinderte lernen gemeinsam. Handbuch der Integrationspädagogik. Weinheim/Basel 1990 (2. Aufl.).

EGGERT, D./KIPHARD, E.J.: Die Bedeutung der Motorik für die Entwicklung normaler und behinderter Kinder. Schorndorf 1980.

EHNI, H./KRETSCHER, J./SCHERLER, K.: Spiel und Sport mit Kindern. Hamburg 1985

FEDIUK, F.: Bewegung, Spiel und Sport geistig Behinderter. Teil 1: Kassel 1990.

FEDIUK, F.: Einführung in den Integrationssport. Teil 1: Pädagogisch-konzeptionelle-Grundlagen. Kassel 1992.

FEDIUK, F.: Einführung in den Integrationssport. Teil 2: Spielen in integrativen Gruppen. Kassel 1992.

FUNKE, J. (Hrsg.): Sportunterricht als Körpererfahrung. Reinbeck 1983.

SCHUCAN-KAISER, R.: 1010 Spiel- und Übungsformen für Behinderte (und Nichtbehinderte). Schorndorf 1986.

SCHUCHARD, E.: Schritte aufeinander zu, Soziale Integration Behinderter durch Weiterbildung. Bad Heilbrunn 1987.

SEIFERT, K. H./STANGL, W.: Einstellung zu Körperbehinderten und ihre beruflich-soziale Integration. Bern 1981.

SEYWALD, A.: Körperliche Behinderung, Grundfragen einer Soziologie der Benachteiligten. Frankfurt a. M. 1977.

SPECK, O.: Geistige Behinderung und Erziehung. München/Basel 1980.

SPECK, O.: System Heipädagogik. München/Basel 1988.

SPECK, O./MARTIN, K.-R. (Hrsg.): Handbuch der Sonderpädagogik und Sozialarbeit. Berlin 1990.

STEINER, G.: Zur Situation Körperbehinderter in der Bundesrepublik von 1945 bis heute. In: Interessengemeinschaft behinderter Studenten Berlin (Hrsg.): Erfahrungsaustausch behinderter Studenten in Ost und West Tagung 90. Berlin 1990, 55-78.

THIMM, W.: Das Normalisierungsprinzip – Eine Einführung. Marburg 1984.

THUST, W.: Die Rechte der Behinderten und ihrer Angehörigen. Düsseldorf 1980.

VERMEER, A.: Der Einfluß von Sport auf die persönliche Kompetenz und soziale Stellung von geistig Behinderten. In: MOTORIK 11 (1988) 1, 17-24.

VON BRACKEN, H.: Vorurteile gegen behinderte Kinder, ihre Familien und Schulen. Berlin 1976.

WURZEL, B.: Sportunterricht mit Behinderten und Nichtbehinderten. Schorndorf 1991.

ZIELNIOK, W.J./SCHMIDT-THIMME, D.: Gestaltete Freizeit mit geistig Behinderten. Rheinstetten 1979 (2. Aufl.).

ZIELNIOK, W.J./ KLÖCKNER, G.: Ergebnisse einer Expertenbefragung zur Freizeitförderung im Bereich der Rehabilitation Behinderter. In: ZIELNIOK, W.J./ SCHMIDT-THIMME, D.: Gestaltete Freizeit mit geistig Behinderten. Rheinstetten 1979 (2. Aufl.), 88-116.

ZIMMER, R./CIRCUS, H.: Psychomotorik. Schorndorf 1987.

ZIMMERMANN, K. W./KAUL, P.: Einführung in die Psychomotorik. Kassel 1989.

2. Practice

ALBERTI, H./ROTHENBERG, L.: Spielreihen in der Spielschulung. Schorndorf 1975.

BAER, U.: Kennenlernspiele – Einstiegsmethoden. Köln o. J.

BAER, U.: Remscheider Spielkartei. Köln o.J.

BAUMGARTEN, M./FARBER, G./MICHELS, F.: SPIKS, Spielkartei für Sonder- und Heilpädagogik. Dortmund 1992.

BISCHOPS, K./GERHARDS, H.-W.: Tips für Sportspiele. Aachen 1987.

BISCHOPS, K./GERHARDS, H.-W.: Tips für Feiern in Sport und Freizeit. Aachen 1988.

BORT, W.: Spiele, nicht nur für Rollstuhlfahrer. Bochum o.J.

BRINKMANN, A./TREES, U.: Bewegungsspiele. Reinbek 1980.

BUCHER, W. (Hrsg.): 1010 Spiel- und Übungsformen für Behinderte (und Nichtbehinderte). Schorndorf 1986.

BUCHER, W. u.a.: 1001 Spielformen im Wasser. Schorndorf 1976.

CRATTY, B.J.: Aktive Spiele und soziales Lernen. Ravensburg 1981.

DEUTSCHER FUSSBALLBUND: Mit kleinen Spiele zum großen Spiel. Frankfurt o.J.

Please order our catalogue!

IAAF/
Gert-Peter Brüggemann (ed.)
**Biomechanical
Research Project**

ISBN 1-84126-009-6
DM 39,80/SFr 37,-/ÖS 291,-
£ 15.-/US$ 24.-
Austr.$ 37.95/Can$ 39.95

Maurice Roche (ed.)
CSRC Edition Volume 5

Sport, Popular Culture and Identity

SBN 3-89124-468-1
DM 29,80/SFr 27,70/ÖS 218,-
£ 12.95/US $ 17.95
Austr.$ 29.95/Can$25.95

SLPE Volume 3
Merkel/ Tokarski (eds.)
**Racism and
Xenophobia in
European Football**

ISBN 3-89124-343-X
DM 29,80/SFr 27,70/ÖS 218,-
£ 12.95/US$ 17.95
Austr.$ 29.95/Can$ 25.95

de Knop/ Theeboom/
van Puymbroeck (et. al.)
**Recreational Games
and Tournaments**

ISBN 3-89124-446-0
DM 29,80/SFr 27,70/ÖS 218,-
£12.95/US$ 17.95
Austr.$ 29.95/Can$ 25.95

Sugden/Bairner (eds.)
CSRC Edition Volume 4

**Sport in Divided
Societies**

ISBN 3-89124-445-2
DM 29,80/SFr 27,70/ÖS 218,-
£ 12.95/US $ 17.95
Austr.$ 29.95/Can$ 25.95

SLPE Volume 2
Doll-Tepper/Brettschneider(eds.)
**Physical Education and
Sport - Changes and
Challenges**

ISBN 3-89124-320-0
DM 39,80/ SFr 37,-/ÖS 291,-
£ 17.95/US$ 29.-
Austr.$37.95/Can$ 39.95

Mike Lowe
CSRC Edition Volume 8

**Dance and Rave
Cultures** ●

ISBN 1-84126–020-7
DM 29,80/SFr 27,70/ÖS 218,-
£ 12.95/US$ 17.95
Austr.$ 29.95/Can$ 25.95

Alan Tomlinson (ed.)
CSRC Edition Volume 3

**Gender, Sport and
Leisure**

ISBN 3-89124-443-6
DM 34,-/SFr 31,60/ÖS 248,-
£ 14.95/US $ 24.-/ Austr. $
32.95/Can $ 34.95

SLPE Volume 1
**Sport Sciences in
Europe 1993 —
Current and Future
Perspectives**

ISBN 3-89124-222-0
DM 39,80/SFr 37,-/ÖS 291,-
£ 17.95/US$ 29.-
Austr.$ 37.95/Can$ 39.95

Graham McFee (ed.)
CSRC Edition Volume 7

**Dance, Education and
Philosophy**

ISBN 1-84126–008-8
DM 29,80/SFr 27,70/ÖS 218,-
£ 12.95/US$ 17.95
Austr.$ 29.95/Can$ 25.95

McFee/Tomlinson (eds.)
CSRC Edition Volume 2

**Education, Sport and
Leisure**

ISBN 3-89124-442-8
DM 29,80/SFr 27,70/ÖS 218,-
£ 12.95/US $ 17.95
Austr.$ 29.95/Can$ 25.95

ISCPES
Hardman/ Standeven
**Cultural Diversity and
Congruence in PE and Sport**

ISBN 3-89124-557-2
DM 39,80/ SFr 37,-/ÖS 291,-
£ 17.95/US$ 29.-
Austr.$37.95/Can$ 39.95

Lincoln Allison (ed.)
CSRC Edition Volume 6
Taking Sport Seriously

ISBN 3-89124-479-7
DM 29,80/SFr 27,70/ÖS 218,-
£ 14.95/US $ 17.95
Austr.$ 28.95/Can$ 25.95

Tomlinson/Fleming (eds.)
CSRC Edition Volume 1
**Ethics, Sport and
Leisure**

ISBN 3-89124-441-X
DM 34,-/SFr 31,60/ÖS 248,-
£ 14.95/US $ 24.-
Austr. $ 32.95/Can $ 34.95

ICSSPE/ **Perspectives – The**
Multidisciplinary Series of PE
and Sport Science /Vol. 1
**Competition in
School Sport**
ISBN 1-84126-019-3
DM 29,80/SFr 27,70/ÖS 218/£14.95
US$ 19.95/Austr.$ 29.95/Can$ 29.95

MEYER & MEYER SPORT

Order worldwide: Great Britain/Ireland: Windsor Books International Fax: 0044/ 18 65 361 133
Canada: Prologue Fax: 001-450 434 2627
Australia/New Zealand: Bookwise International Fax: 00618/ 8268/ 8704
USA: Partners Book Distributing, Inc. Fax: 001-517-694-0617

Our Programme

Gudrun Paul
Aerobic Training

ISBN 1-84126-021-5
DM 29,80/SFr 27,70/ÖS 218,-
£ 12.95/US$ 17.95
Austr.$ 29.95/Can$ 25.95

Unger/Rössler
Bodywork –
Power for Women

ISBN 1-84126-022-3
DM 29,80/SFr 27,70/ÖS 218,-
£ 12.95/US$ 17.95
Austr.$ 29.95/Can$ 25.95

Diel/Menges
Surfing
In search of the perfect wave

ISBN 1-84126-023-1
DM 29.80/SFr 27,70/ÖS 218,-
£ 12.95/US $ 17.95
Austr. $ 29.95/Can $ 25.95

Wolfgang Fritsch
Rowing

ISBN 1-84126-024-X
DM 34 ,-/SFr 31,60/ÖS 248,-
£ 14.95/US$ 19.95
Austr.$ 29.95/Can$ 29.95

Green/Hardman (eds.)
Physical Education
A Reader

ISBN 3-89124-463-0
DM 39,80/SFr 37,-/ÖS 291,-
£ 17.95/US $ 29,-
Austr.$ 37.95/ Can$ 39.95

Arthur Lydiard revolutionised the training of middle and long distance runners in the 1960s. Since then his methods have contributed to the success of countless athletes around the world, including four time Olympic gold medalist and world record setter Lasse Viren of Finland.

Lydiard/Gilmour
Distance Training for
Women Athletes

ISBN 1-84126-002-9
DM 24,80/SFr 23,-/ÖS 181,-
£ 9.95/US$ 14.95
Austr.$ 24.95/Can$ 20.95

Lydiard Gilmour
Distance Training for
Masters

ISBN 1-84126-018-5
c. DM 29,80/SFr 27,70/ÖS 218,-
£ 12.95/US$ 17.95
Austr.$ 29.95/Can$ 25.95

Lydiard/Gilmour
Distance Training for
Young Athletes

ISBN 3-89124-533-5
DM 29,80/SFr 27,70/ÖS 218,-
£ 12.95/US$ 17.95
Austr.$ 29.95/Can$ 25.95

Arthur Lydiard
Running to the Top

ISBN 3-89124-440-1
DM 29,80/SFr 27,70/ÖS 218,-
£ 12.95/US$ 17.95
Austr.$ 29.95/Can$ 25.95

Do you want to improve your training? – Let Lydiard be your personal coach!
For US$ 240,- /year only Lydiard offers you personal training plans and advice.

For more information turn to

www.lydiard.com

or

www.meyer-meyer-sports.com

MEYER
& MEYER
SPORT

SCHUHMACHER, E.: Singspiele und Kindertänze für die Grundschule. Schorndorf 1972.

SCHWEIHER, G.: Komm mit, spiel mit – Bd. 1: In der Gruppe erprobte Spiele. Mainz 1979.

SCHWEIHER, G.: Komm mit, spiel mit – Bd. 2: Spiele für Freizeit, Fahrt und Lager. Mainz 1980.

SILBER, H.-P./RIEMER, CH./KUHN, M./ERNI, CH.: Spiele ohne Sieger. Ravensburg 1976.

SPORTJUGEND HESSEN (Hrsg.): Integrativer Freizeitsport. Frankfurt a.M. 1990.

SPORTJUGEND HESSEN (Hrsg.): Bewegung Kunterbunt, Spiel und Sport für behinderte und nichtbehinderte Kinder. Frankfurt 1992 (2. Aufl.).

SPORTPÄDAGOGIK: Spiele 1 (1980).

SPORTPÄDAGOGIK: Bewegungsspiele 1 (1983).

STIFF, G.: 1000 Jugendspiele. Münster o.J.

STÜND, H.: Koedukation und kleine Spiele. Schorndorf 1979.

VATER, W.: Spiele für Urlaub, Reise und Freizeit. Eine Spielesammlung für gesunde und behinderte Kinder. Bonn 1983.

WIEMANN, K.: Spiel mit. Limpert-Verlag 1967.

WOESLER, D. M.: Spiele, Feste, Gruppenprogramm. Frankfurt a.M. 1978.

ZALFEN, W.: Spielräume. Über 100 Vorschläge für Spiel, Bewegung, Kommunikation. Mainz 1988.

ZIMMER, R.: Kreative Bewegungsspiele, Psychomotorische Förderung im Kindergarten. Freiburg 1990.

ZUCKRIGL, H. U. A./HELBING, H.: Rhythmik hilft behinderten Kinder. München 1988.

Our Programme

Jozef Sneyers
Soccer Training
An Annual Programme

ISBN 1-84126-017-7
c. DM 34 ,-/SFr 31,60/ÖS 248,-
£ 12.95/US$ 19.95
Austr.$ 29.95/Can$ 29.95

Gerhard Frank
Soccer Training Programmes

ISBN 3-89124-556-4
DM 29,80/SFr 27,70/ÖS 218,-
£ 12.95/US$ 17.95
Austr.$ 29.95/Can$ 25.95

Ilona E. Gerling
Teaching Children's Gymnastics

ISBN 3-89124-549-1
DM 29,80/SFr 27,70/ÖS 218,-
£ 12.95/US $ 17.95
Austr.$ 29.95/Can$ 25.95

Bischops/Gerards
Soccer
Warming-up and Cooling down

ISBN 1-84126-014-2
c. DM 24,80/SFr 23,-/ÖS 181,-
£ 8.95/US$ 14.95
Austr.$24.95/Can$ 20.95

Bischops/Gerards
Junior Soccer:
A Manual for Coaches

ISBN 1-84126-000-2
DM 29,80/SFr 27,70/ÖS 218,-
£ 12.95/US$ 17.95
Austr.$ 29.95/Can$ 25.95

Thomas Kaltenbrunner
Contact Improvisation

ISBN 3-89124-485-1
DM 29,80/SFr 27,70/ÖS 218,-
£ 12.95/US$ 17.95
Austr.$ 29.95/Can$ 25.95

Bischops/Gerards
Soccer
One-On-One

ISBN 1-84126-013-4
c. DM 24,80/SFr 23,-/ÖS 181,-
£ 8.95/US$ 14.95
Austr.$24.95/Can$ 20.95

Bischops/Gerards
Coaching Tips for Children's Soccer

ISBN 3-89124-529-7
DM 14,80/SFr 14,40/ÖS 108,-
£ 5.95/US$ 8.95
Austr.$ 14.95/Can$ 12.95

Dörte Wessel-Therhorn
Jazz Dance Training

ISBN 3-89124-499-1
DM 29,80/SFr 27,70/ÖS 218,-
£ 12.95/US$ 17.95
Austr.$ 29.95/Can$ 25.95

Gerhard Frank
Soccer
Creative Training

ISBN 1-84126-015-0
c. DM 24,80/SFr 23,-/ÖS 181,-
£ 8.95/US$ 14.95
Austr.$24.95/Can$ 20.95

Pieter/Heijmans
Scientific Coaching for Olympic Taekwondo

ISBN 3-89124-389-8
DM 29,80/SFr 27,70/ÖS 218,-
£ 12.95/US$ 17.95
Austr.$ 29.95/Can$ 25.95

Bergmann/Butz
Adventure Sports – Big Foot

ISBN 3-89124-497-5
DM 34 ,-/SFr 31,60/ÖS 248,-
£ 14.95/US$ 19.95
Austr.$ 29.95/Can$ 29.95

Erich Kollath
Soccer
Techniques & Tactics

ISBN 1-84126-016-9
c. DM 24,80/SFr 23,-/ÖS 181,-
£ 8.95/US$ 14.95
Austr.$24.95/Can$ 20.95

Rudolf Jakhel
Modern Sports Karate

ISBN 3-89124-428-2
DM 29,80/SFr 27,70/ ÖS 218,-
£ 12.95/US$ 17.95
Austr.$ 29.95/Can$ 25.95

Münch/ Mund
Straight Golf

ISBN 3-89124-503-3
DM 34,-/SFr 31,60/ÖS 248,-
£ 12.95/US$ 19.95
Austr.$ 29.95/Can$ 25.95

● In preparation

MEYER
& MEYER
SPORT

DEUTSCHER SPORTBUND/ELSTNER, F.:Spiel mit. Das große Spielbuch des DSB. Dortmund/Gütersloh 1979.

DEUTSCHER SPORTBUND (Hrsg.): Bewegung, Spiel und Sport mit geistig behinderten Kindern – eine Elterfibel, Bd. 25 der Schriftenreihe Breitensport. Frankfurt 1982.

DEUTSCHER SPORTBUND: 10 Spiele/100 Variationen, Bd. 20 der Schriftenreihe Breitensport. Frankfurt 1982.

DEUTSCHER SPORTBUND: Spielfest, Bd. 18 der Schriftenreihe Breitensport. Frankfurt 1982.

DIERICH, K./LANDAU, G. (Hrsg.): Sportspiele. Reinbek 1985.

DIETRICH, K./DÜRRWÄCHTER, G./SCHALLER, H.-J.: Die großen Spiele. Wuppertal 1978.

DÖBLER, E. u. H.: Kleine Spiel. Berlin-Ost 1975.

FAHNEMANN, A.: Die großen Wasserspiele. Bockenem 1981.

FEDER, J.: Die schönsten Kinderspiele im Freien. München/Zürich 1982.

FLÜGELMANN, A.: New Games – die neuen Spiele. München Bd. 1/1979, Bd. 2/1983.

FLURI, H.: 1012 Spiele und Übungsformen in der Freizeit. Schorndorf 1984.

FRESEN, U.: Risenspaß mit neuen Spielen. München 1986.

GEISSLER, A.: Freudvolle Spiele für das 1. bis 10. Schuljahr. Limpert-Verlag 1977.

HAASE, J.: Spiele im, am, unter Wasser. Berlin 1979.

HAGEDORN, G./BISANZ, G./DUELL, H.: Sport in der Primarstufe, Bd. 3, Das Mannschaftsspiel. Frankfurt a. M. 1972.

JEHN, M. W.: 28 Kinderspiele aus aller Welt. Lilienthal/Bremen 1989.

JOST, E. (Hrsg.): Spielanregungen – Bewegungsspiele. Reinbek 1985.

KATHOLISCHE JUNGE GEMEINDE (KJG): Songbuch. Düsseldorf 1984 (4. Aufl.).

KERKMANN, K.: Kleine Parteiballspiele. Schorndorf 1975.

KNIETZKO, CH.: Sing-, Kreis-, Finger- und Bewegungsspiele zur Förderung des entwicklungsgestörten und des behinderten Kindes. Ravensburg 1978.

KOCH, K.: Kleine Sportspiele. Schorndorf 1969.

KOCH, K.: (Hrsg.): Einführungsmodelle und Spielreihen für Sportspiele, Teil 1: Prellball-Indiaca-Badminton-Faustball. Schorndorf 1976.

KONZAG, G.: Übungsformen für die Sportspiele. Berlin-Ost 1973.

KREIDLER, H.-D.: Konditionsschulung durch Spiele. Schorndorf 1970.

KRENZ, A.: Spiele(n) mit geistigbehinderten Kindern und Jugendlichen. Weinheim 1986.

KRENZER, R.: Spiele mit behinderten Kindern. Lahr 1983.

LEFOLD, P.: Spielaktionen. Hannover 1979.

LÖSCHER, A.: Kleine Spiele für viele. Berlin-Ost 1976.

LUKACSY, A.: Spiele aus aller Welt. Corvina-Verlag o.J.

MARX, E.: Spiele gür alle im Kindergarten, Vorschule, Hof und Halle. Wuppertal 1978.

MEUSEL, H.: Lauf-, Rauf- und Ballspiele. Limpert-Verlag 1978.

ORLICK, T.: Kooperative Spiele. Weinheim 1982.

PEINEMANN, G.: Spiele im Freien. Wolfenbüttel 1984.

RAMME J./RIESE, H.: Spiele für Viele. Vechelde-Vallstedt 1982.

RIEMER, CH.: Neue Spiele ohne Sieger. Ravensburg 1986.

SCHMIDT, R.: 222 Spiele im Wasser. Aschaffenburg 1980.

Our Programme

Hömberg/Papageorgiou
Handbook for Beach-Volleyball

ISBN 3-89124-322-7
DM 38,-/SFr 35,30/ÖS 278,-
£ 17.95/US$ 29.-
Austr.$ 37.95/Can$ 39.95

Papageorgiou/Spitzley
Volleyball:
A Handbook for Coaches and Players

ISBN 1-84126-005-3
DM 34 ,-/SFr 31,60/ÖS 248,-
£ 14.95/US$ 19.95
Austr.$ 29.95/Can$ 29.95

Georg Neumann
Nutrition in Sport

ISBN 1-84126-003-7
c. DM 34 ,-/SFr 31,60/ ÖS 248,-
£ 12.95/US$ 17.95
Austr.$ 29.95/Can$ 29.95

Bös/Saam
Walking
Fitness and Health through Everyday Activity

ISBN 1-84126-001-0
DM 14,80/SFr 14,40/ÖS 108,-
£ 5.95/US$ 8.95
Austr.$ 14.95/Can$ 12.95

Petracic/Röttgermann/Traenckner
Successful Running

ISBN 1-84126-006-1
DM 24,80/SFr 23,-/ÖS 181,-
£ 9.95/US$ 14.95
Austr.$ 24.95/Can$ 20.95

Neumann/Pfützner/ Berbalk
Successful Endurance Training

ISBN 1-84126-004-5
DM 34 ,-/SFr 31,60/ÖS 248,-
£ 12.95/US$ 17.95
Austr.$ 29.95/Can$ 29.95

Kuno Hottenrott
The Complete Guide to Duathlon Training

ISBN 3-89124-530-0
DM 34 ,-/SFr 31,60/ÖS 248,-
£ 14.95/ US$ 19.95
Austr.$ 29.95/Can$ 29.95

Hermann Aschwer
The Complete Guide to Triathlon Training

ISBN 3-89124-515-7
DM 34 ,-/SFr 31,60/ÖS 248,-
£ 12.95/US$ 19.95
Austr.$ 29.95/Can$ 29.95

Achim Schmidt
Handbook of Competitive Cycling

ISBN 3-89124-509-2
DM 34 ,-/SFr 31,60/ÖS 248,-
£ 12.95/US$ 19.95
Austr.$ 29.95/Can$ 29.95

Achim Schmidt
Mountainbike Training

ISBN 1-84126-007-X
DM 29,80/SFr 27,70/ÖS 218,-
£ 12.95/US$ 17.95
Austr.$ 29.95/Can$ 25.95

Richard Schönborn
Advanced Techniques for Competitive Tennis

ISBN 3-89124-534-3
DM 38.-/SFr 35,30/ÖS 278,-
£17.95/US$ 29.-
Austr. $ 37.95/Can $ 39.95

Lutz Steinhöfel
Training Exercises for Competitive Tennis

ISBN 3-89124-464-9
DM 29,80/SFr 27,70/ÖS 218,-
£12.95/US$ 17.95
Austr.$ 29.95/Can$ 25.95

Dieter Koschel
Allround Fitness
The Beginner's Guide

ISBN 1-84126-011-8
DM 24,80/SFr 23,-/ÖS 181,-
£ 9.95/US $ 14.95
Austr.$ 24.95/Can$ 20.95

Bettina M. Jasper
Train your Brain

Mental and Physical Fitness

ISBN 3-89124-531-9
DM 29,80/SFr 27,70/ÖS 218,-
£12.95/US$ 17.95
Austr.$ 29.95/Can$ 25.95

Uwe Rheker
Integration through Games and Sports

ISBN 1-84126-012-6
DM 29,80/SFr 27,70/ÖS 218,-
£ 12.95/US $ 17.95
Austr.$ 29.95/Can $ 25.95

MEYER & MEYER SPORT

Meyer & Meyer Sport • Von-Coels-Str. 390 • D-52080 Aachen • Fax: 0049241/9 58 10 10

e-mail: verlag@meyer-meyer-sports.com • **Please order by:** www.meyer-meyer-sports.com